To Reach the Source

To Reach the Source

The Stepwells of India

Photographs and Text by Claudio Cambon

with drawings by Tanvi Jain

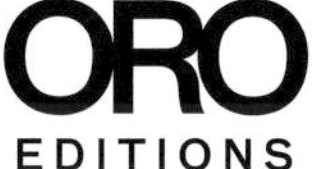

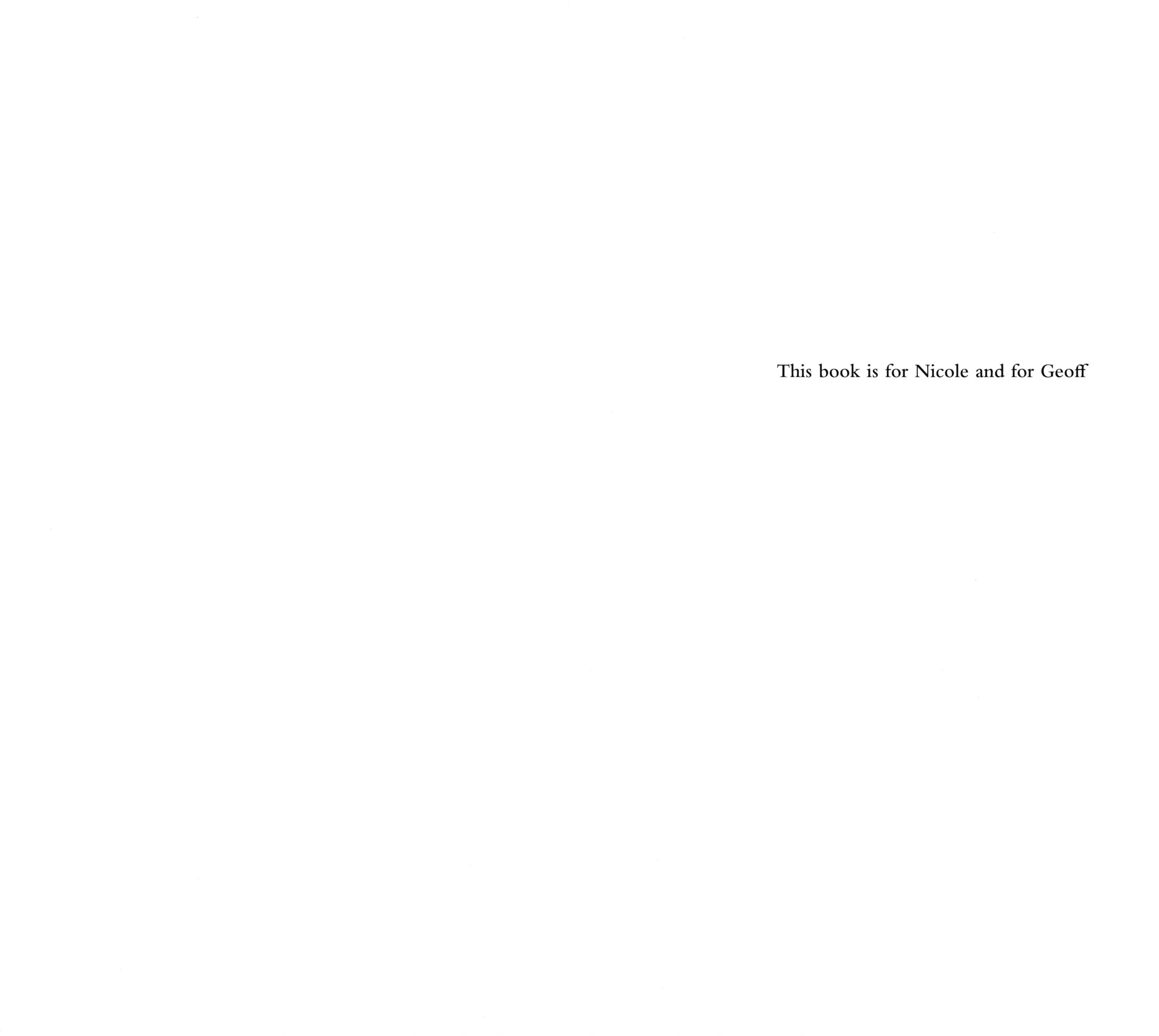

This book is for Nicole and for Geoff

जीवन (jivaná) *n (Sanskrit)*
1. life 2. water, that which gives life

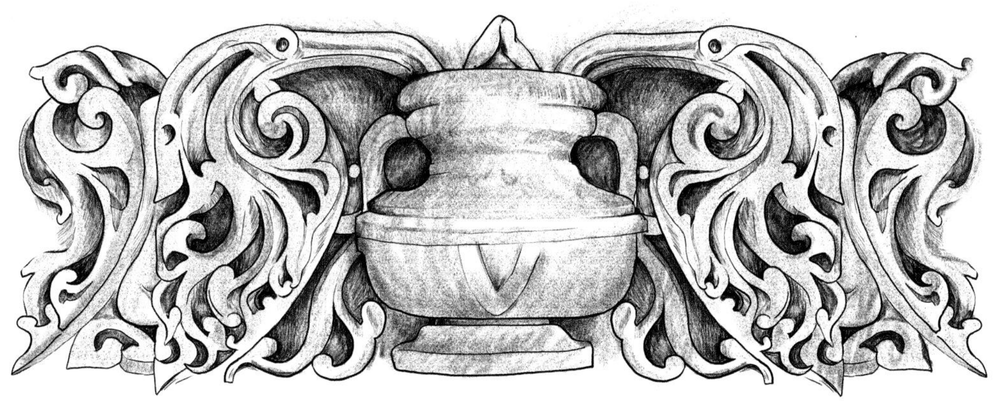

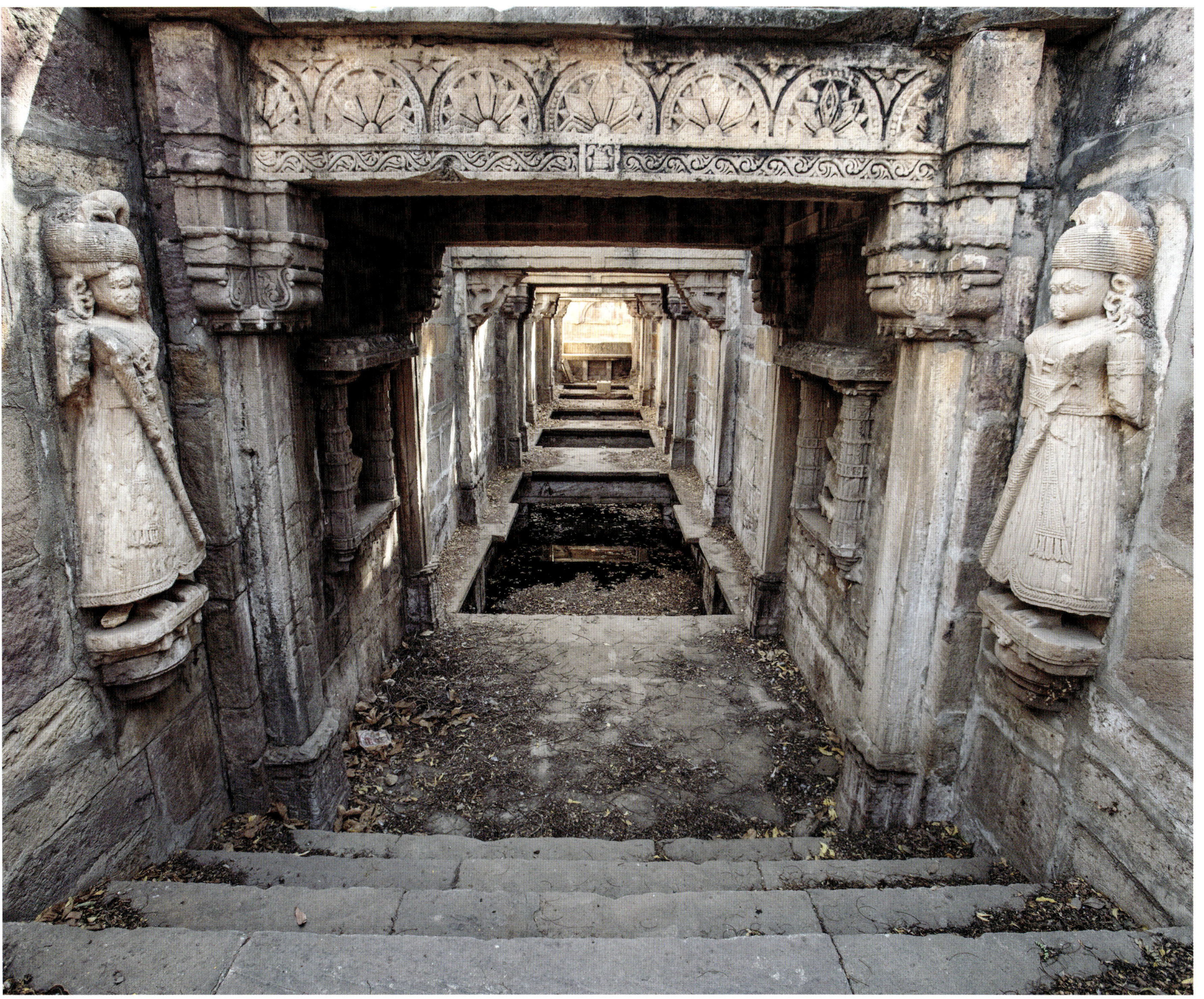

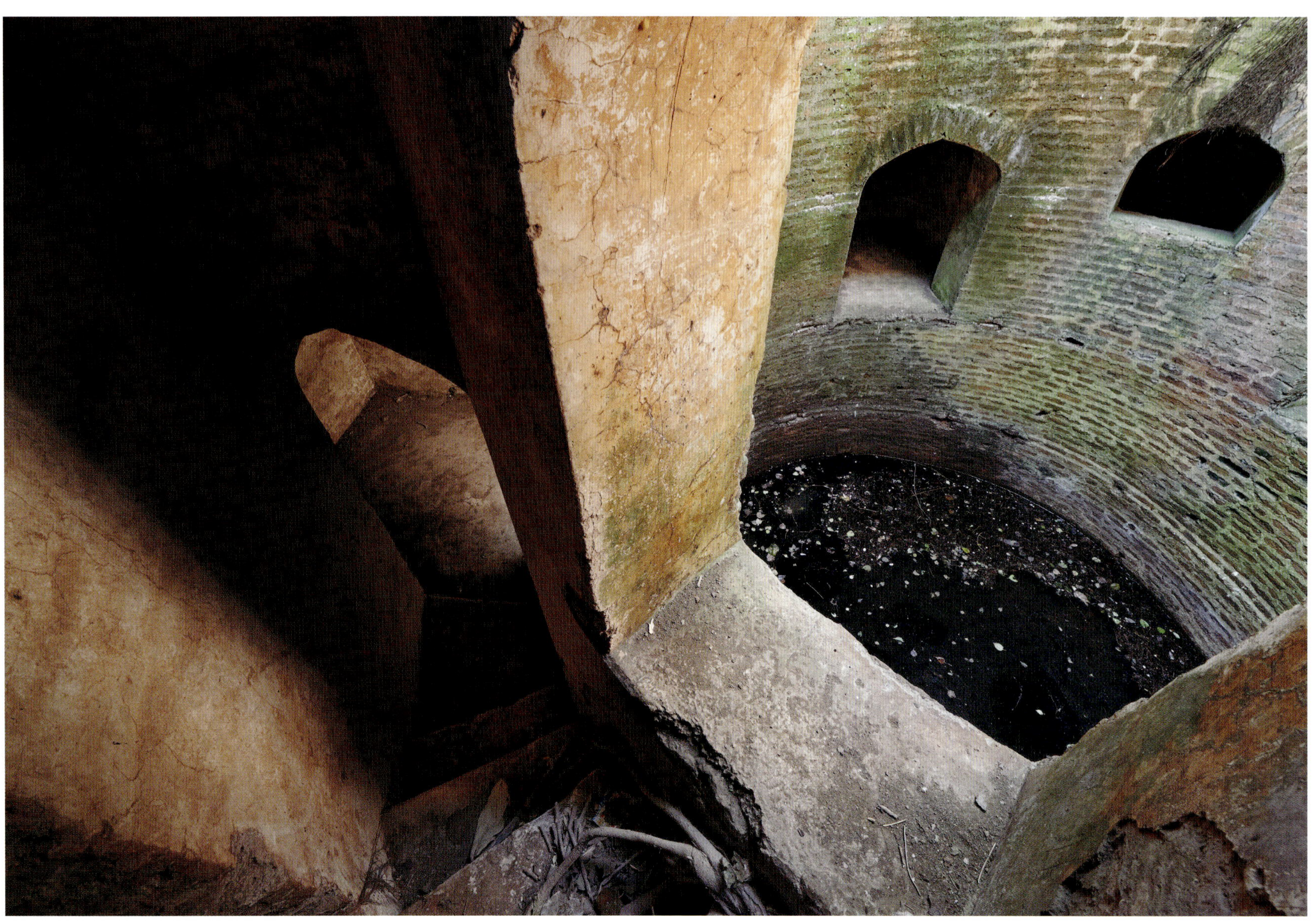

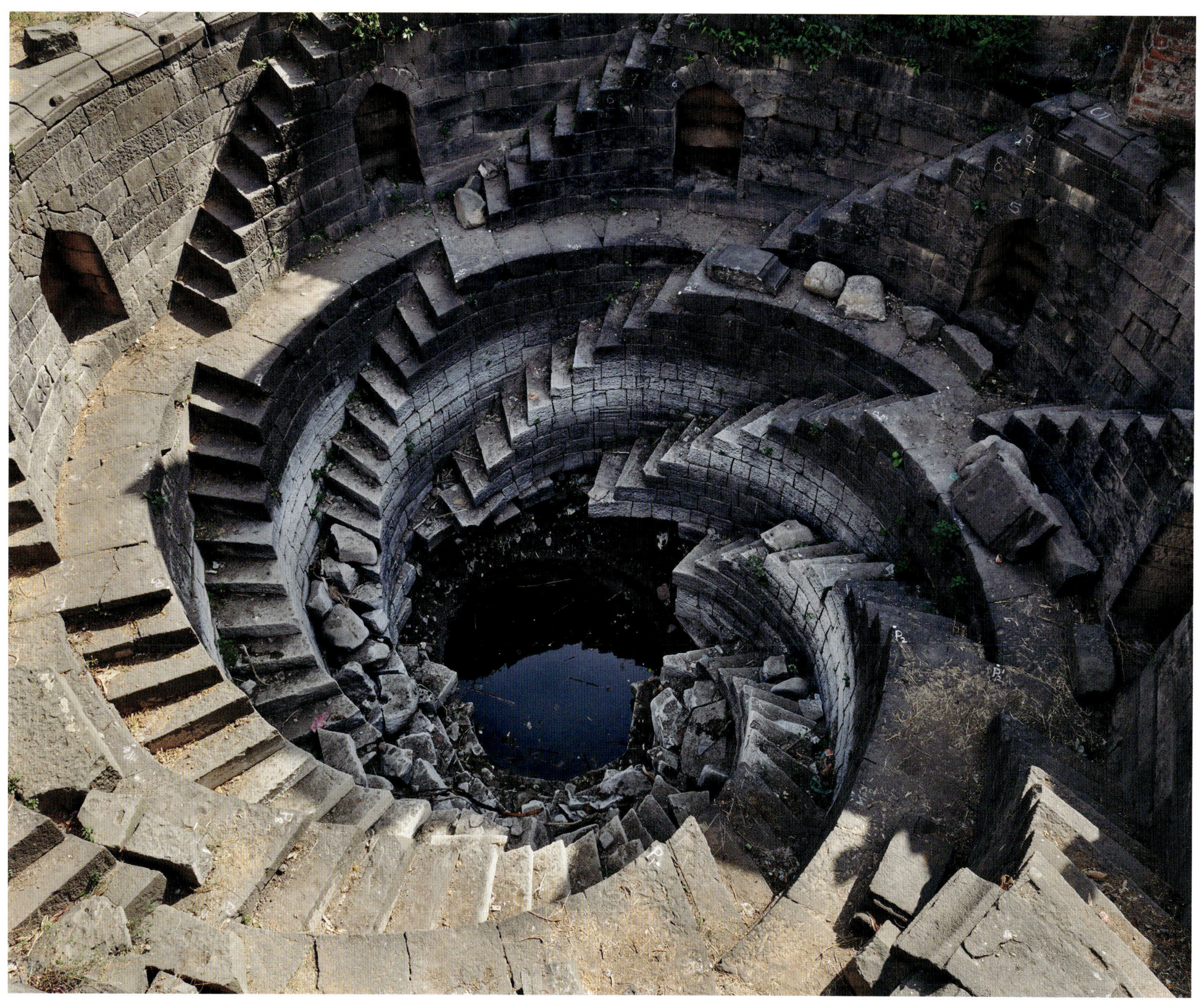

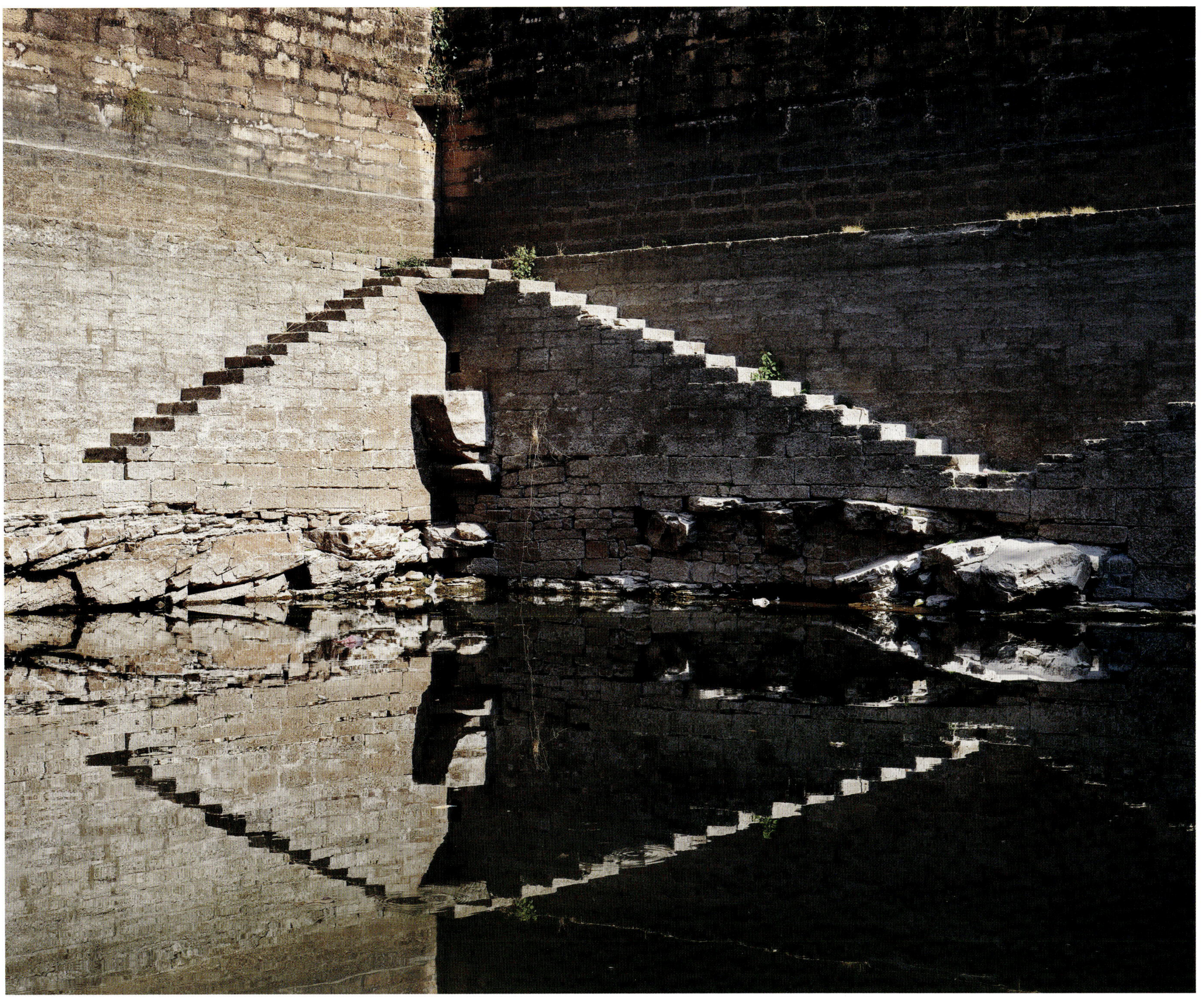

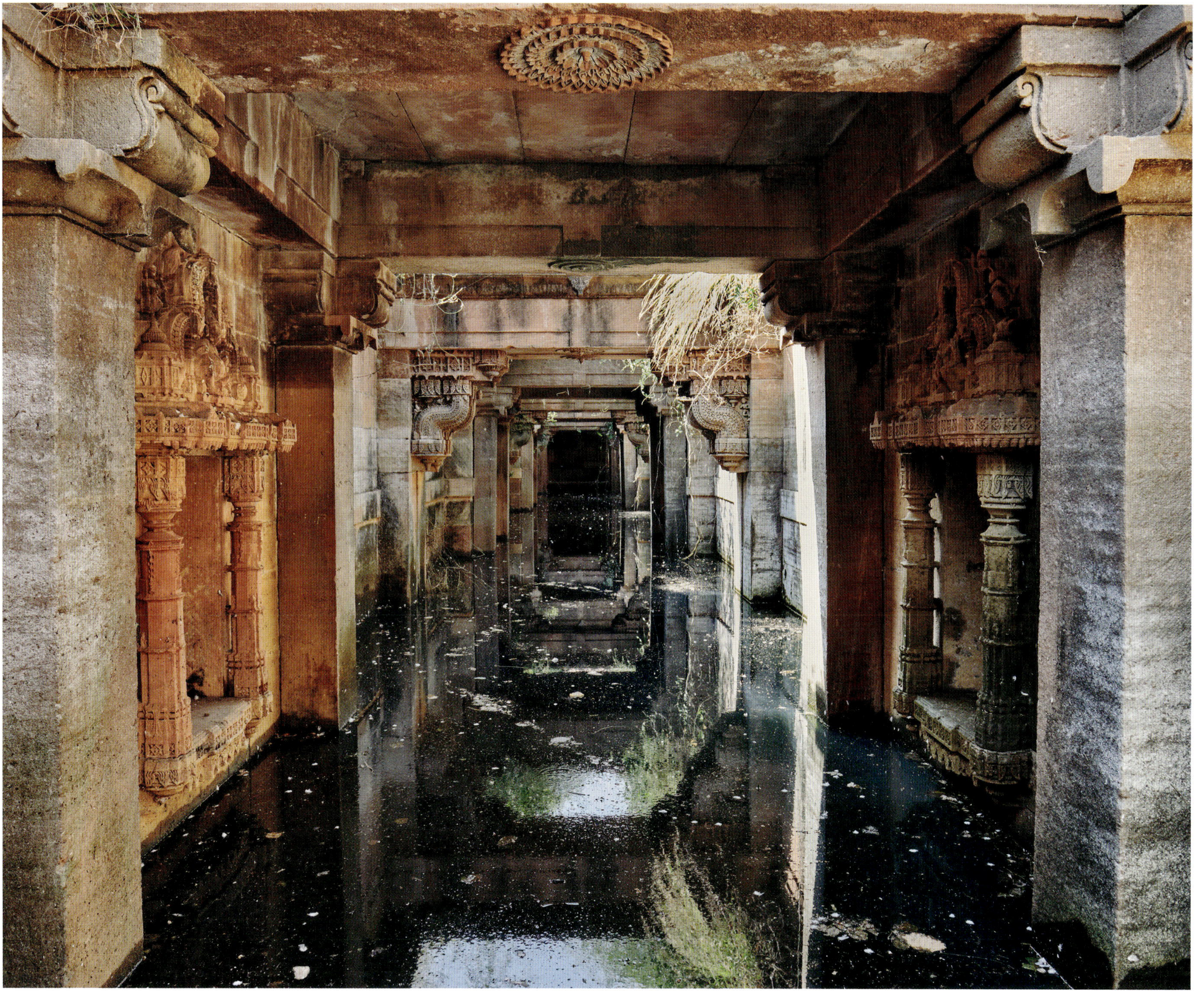

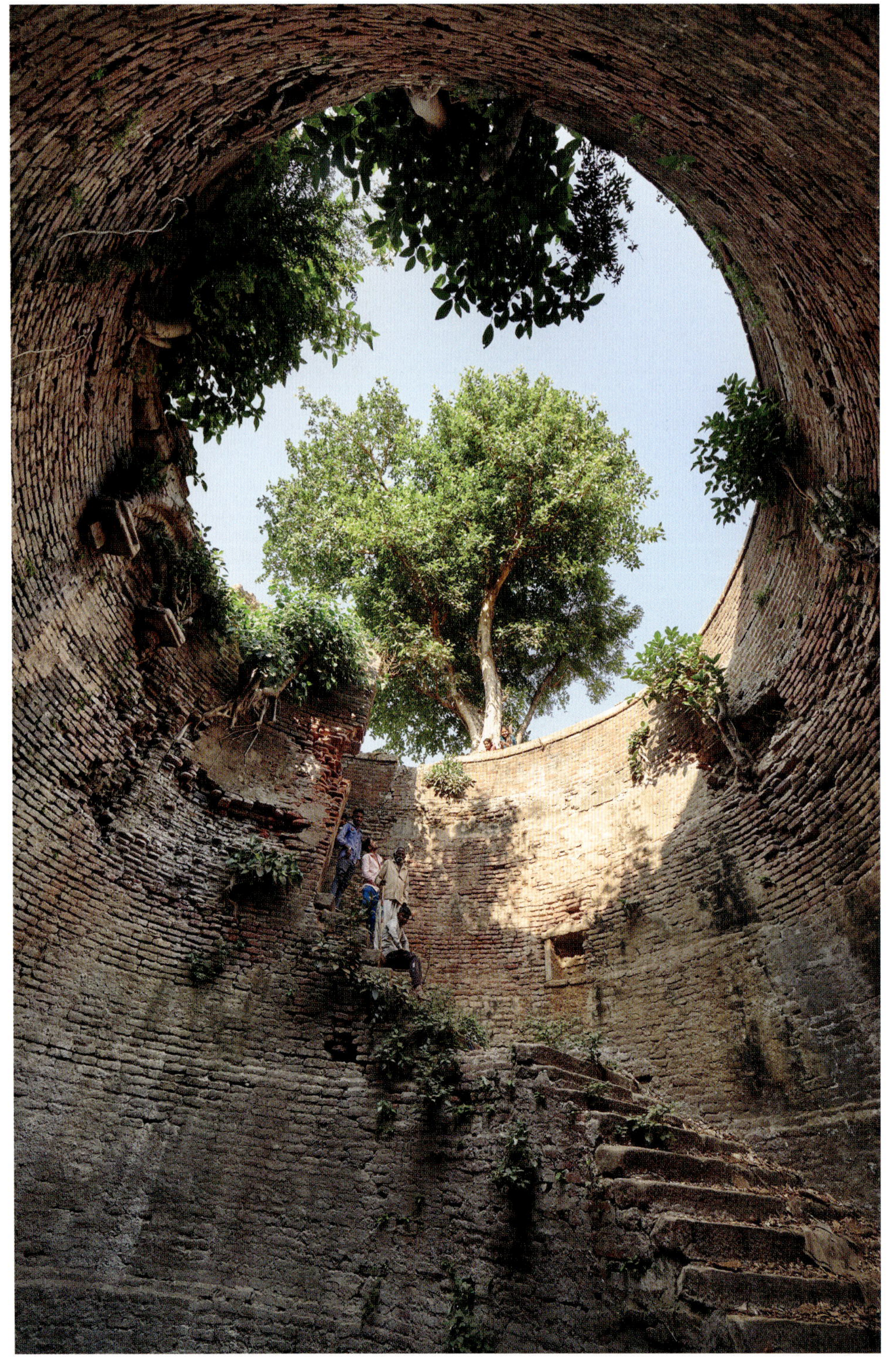

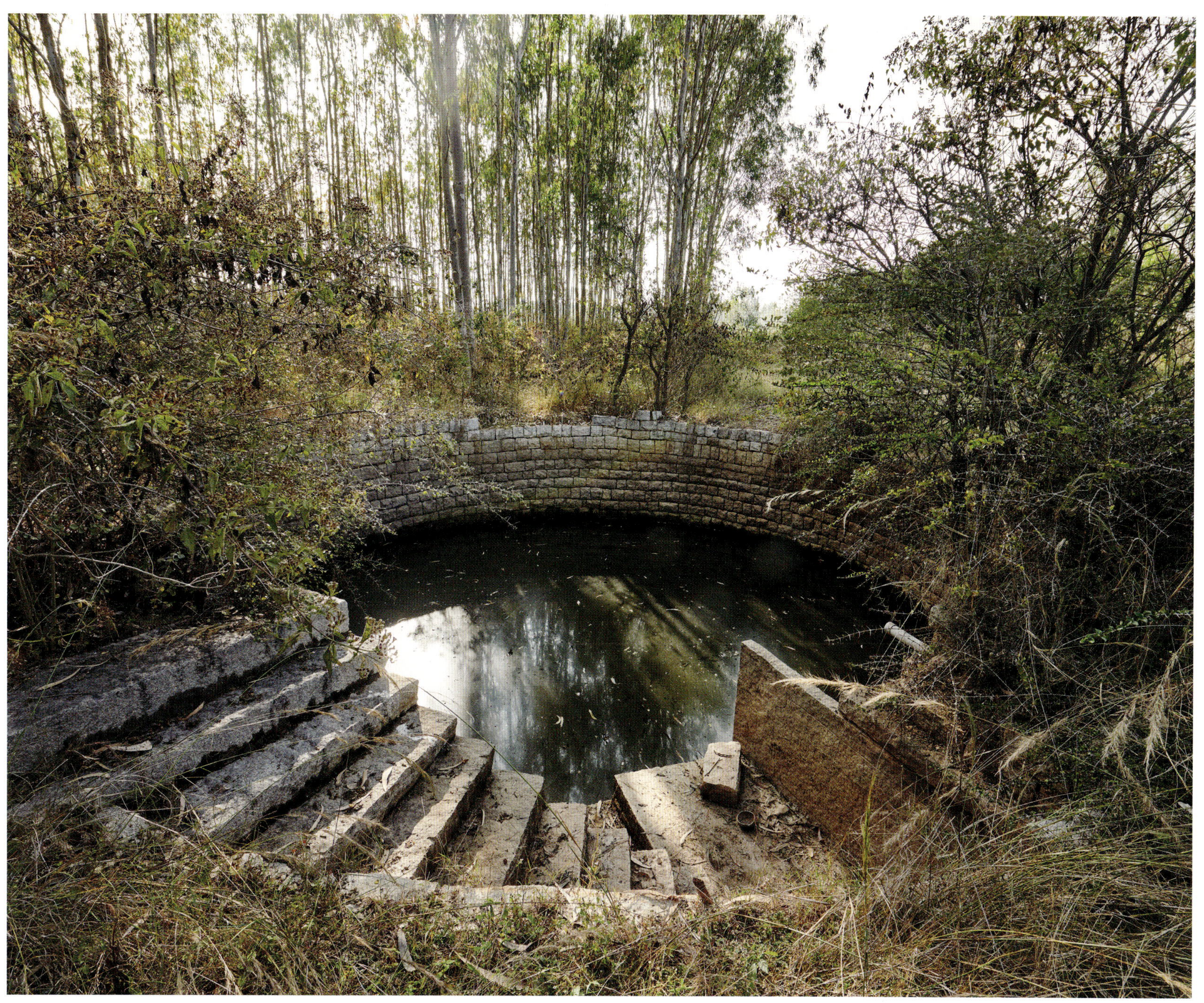

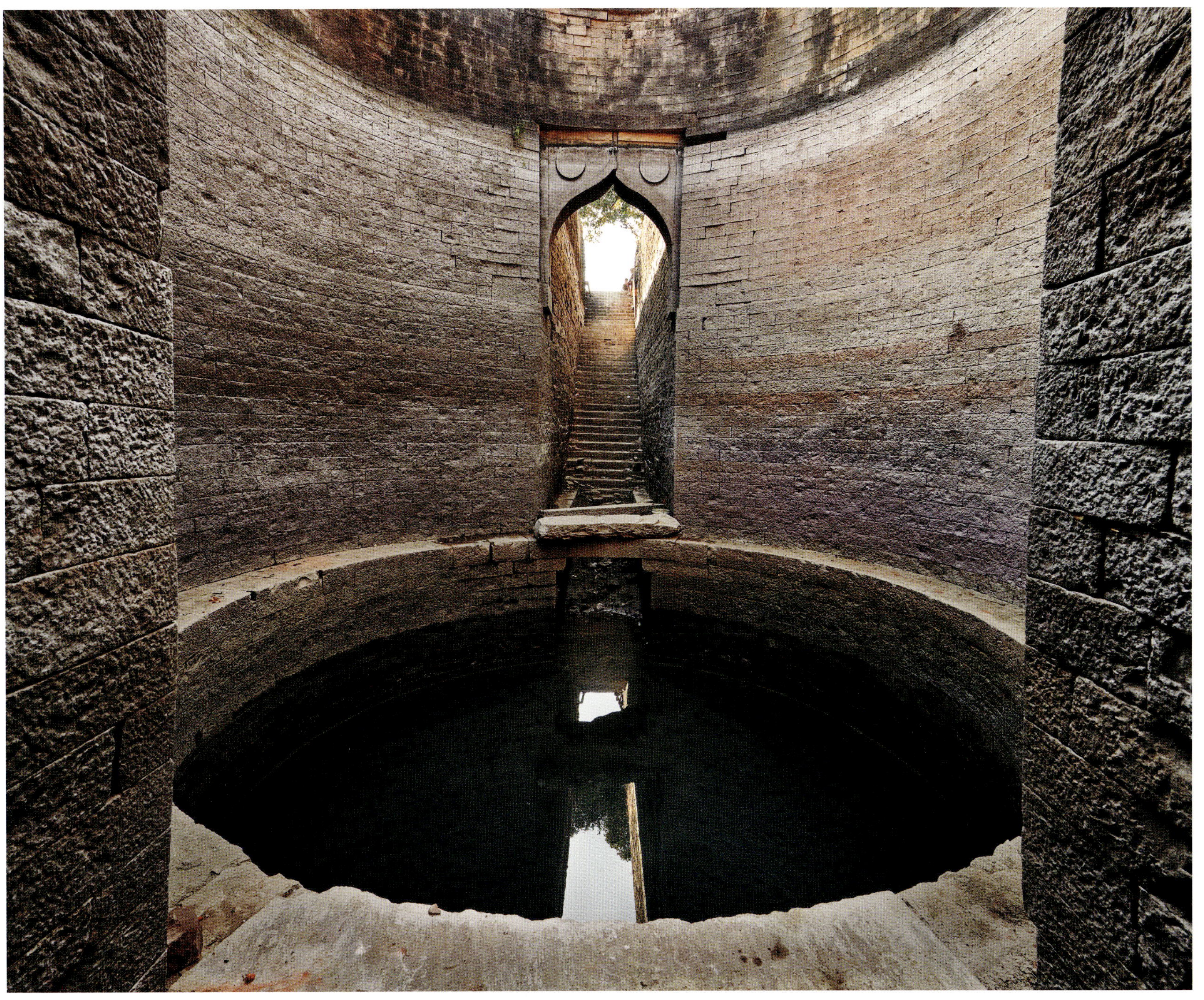

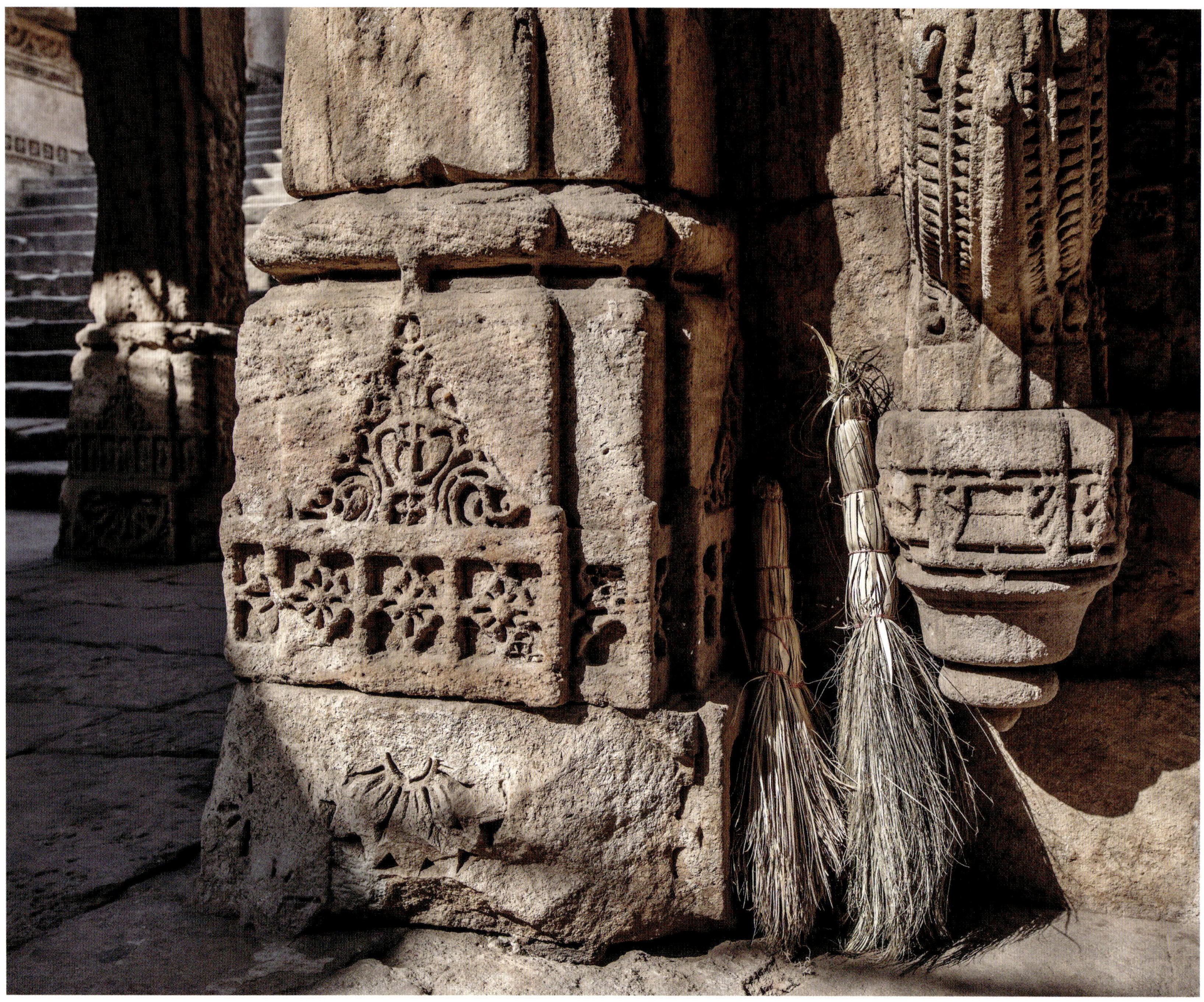

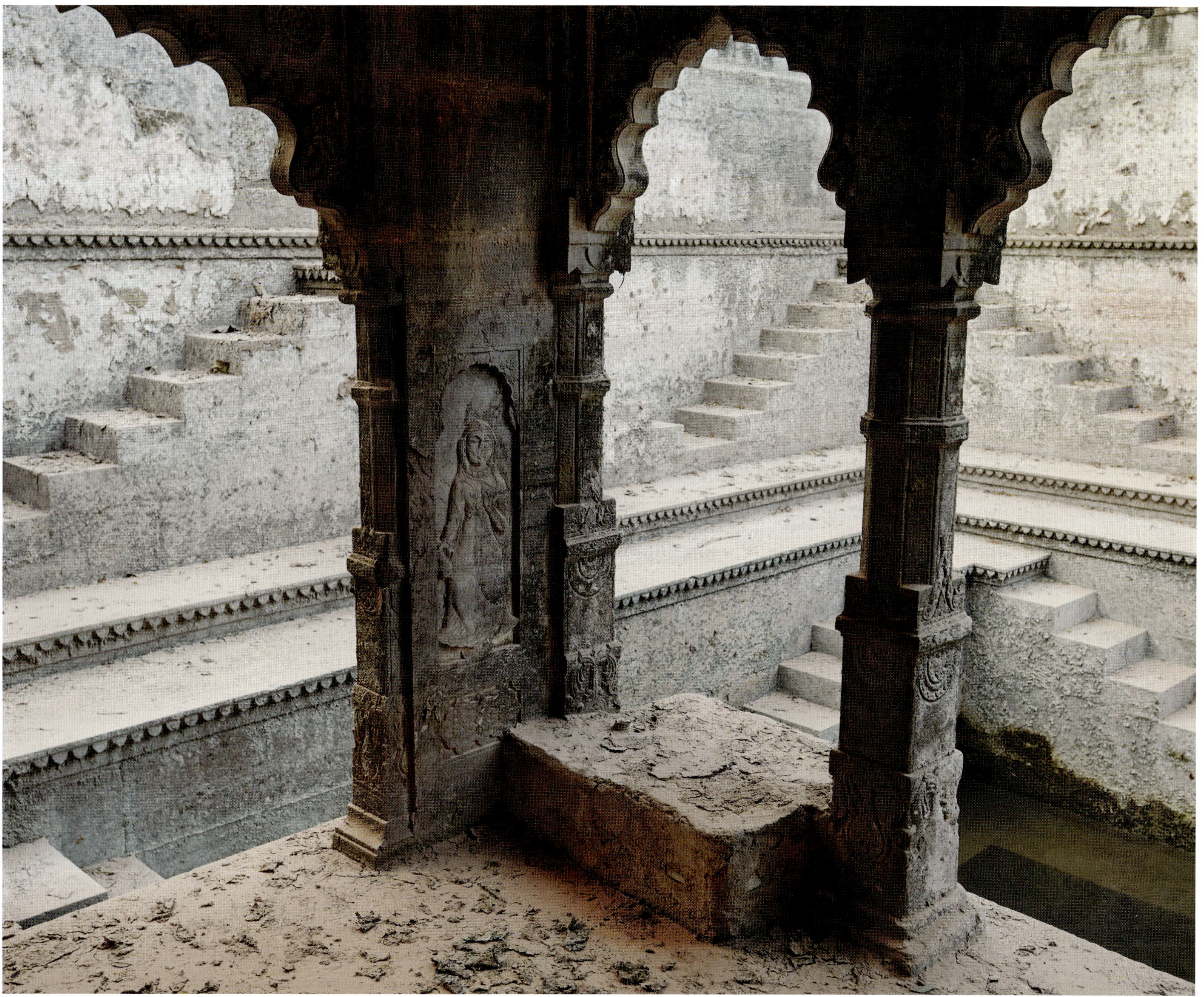

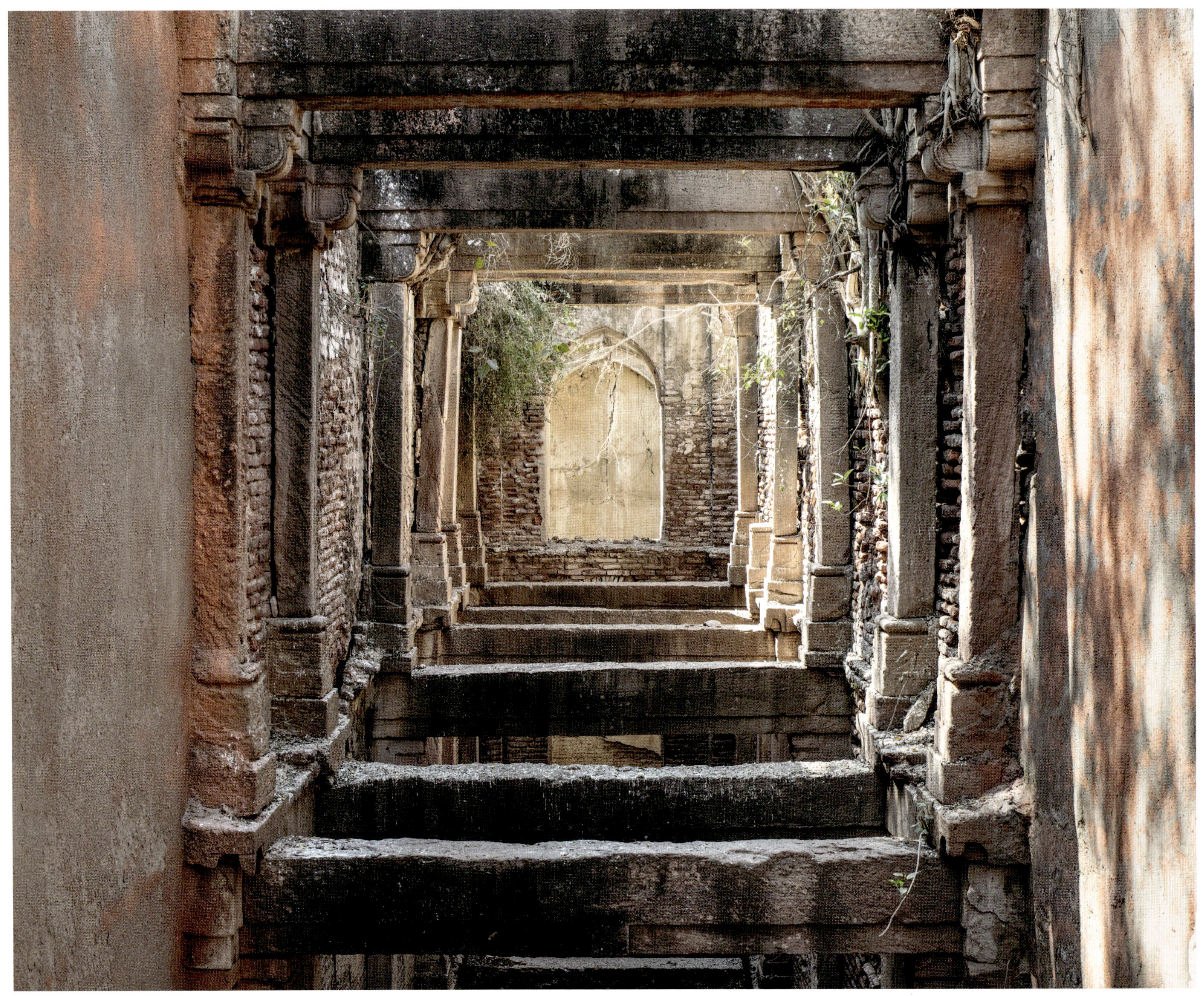

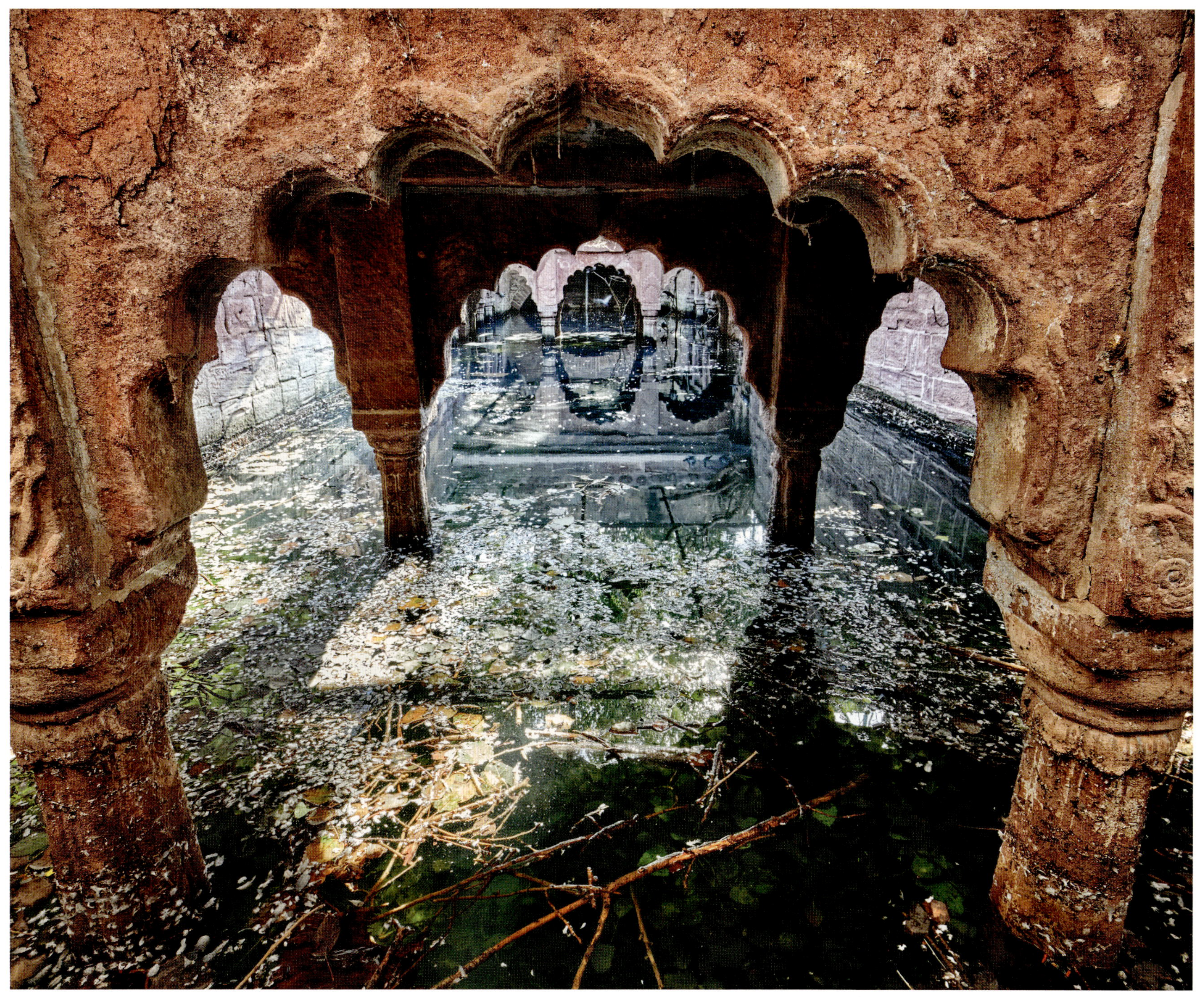

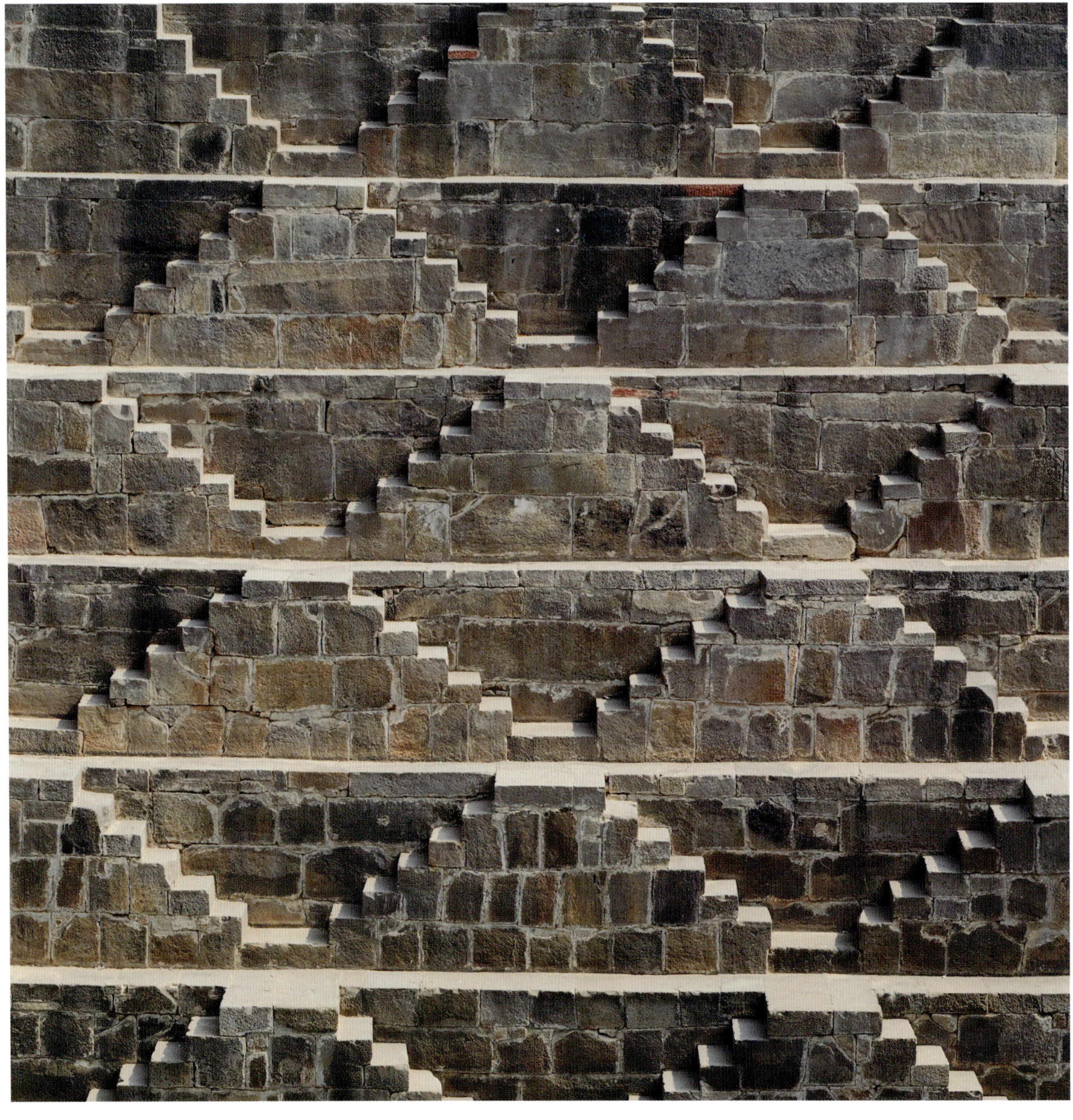

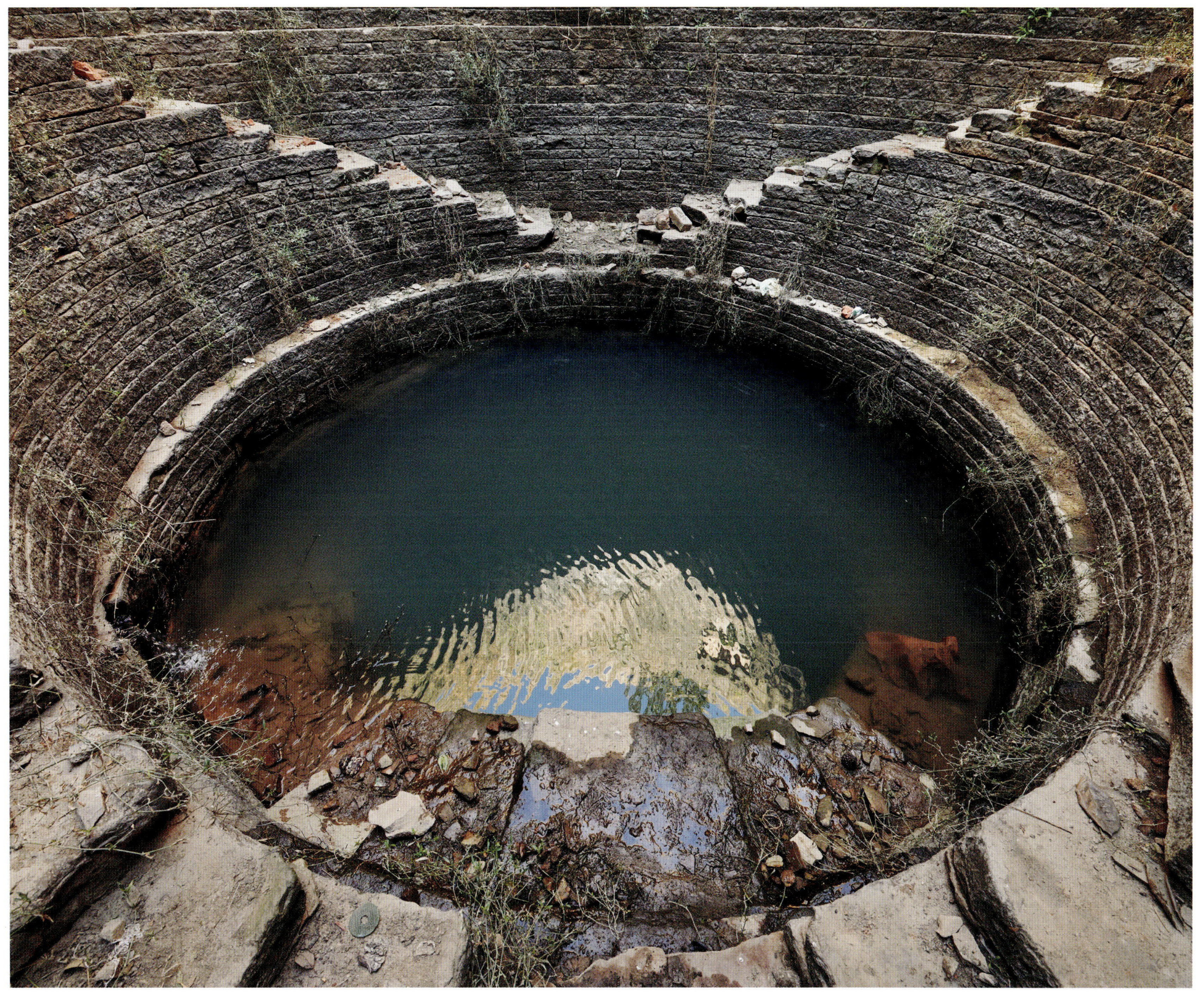

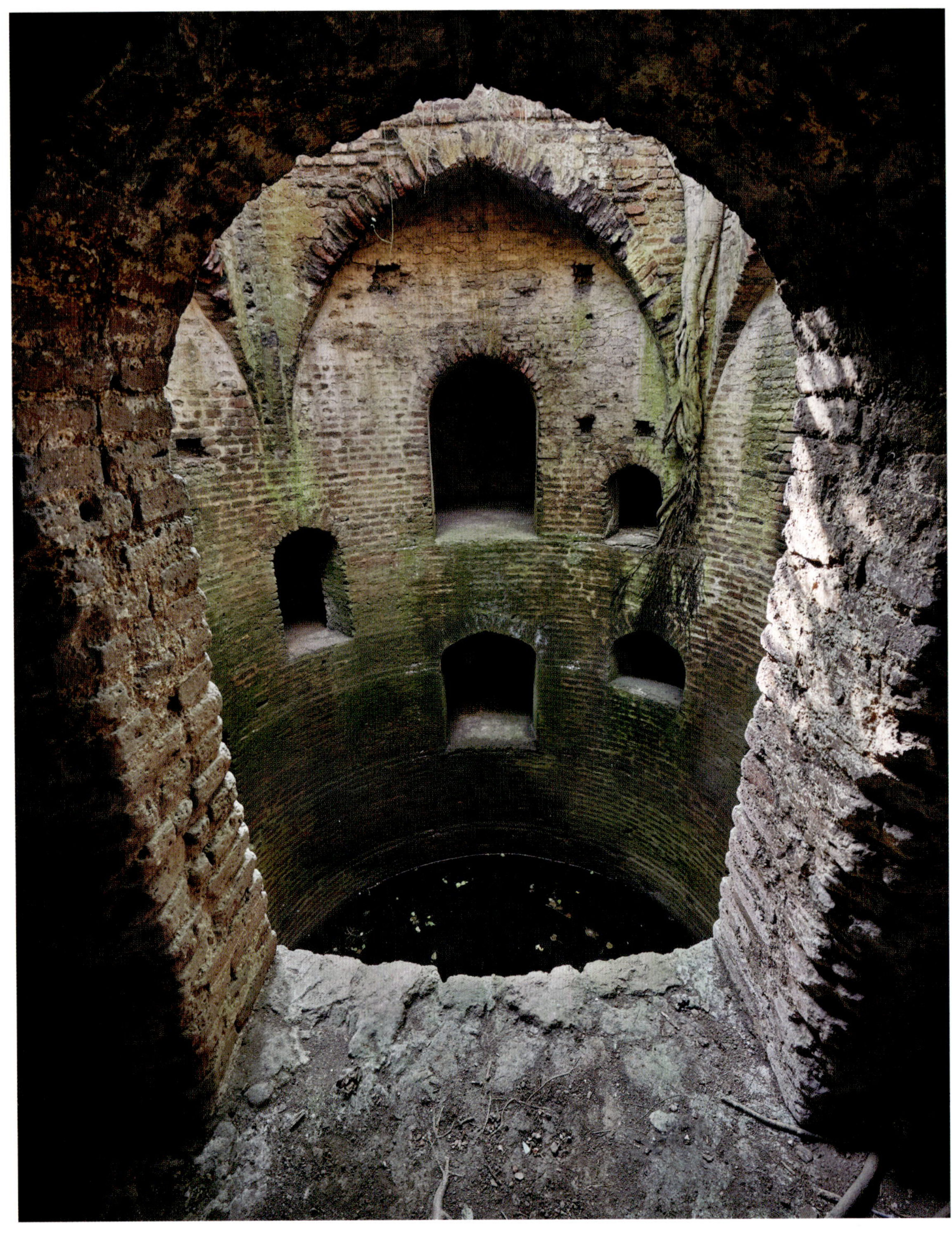

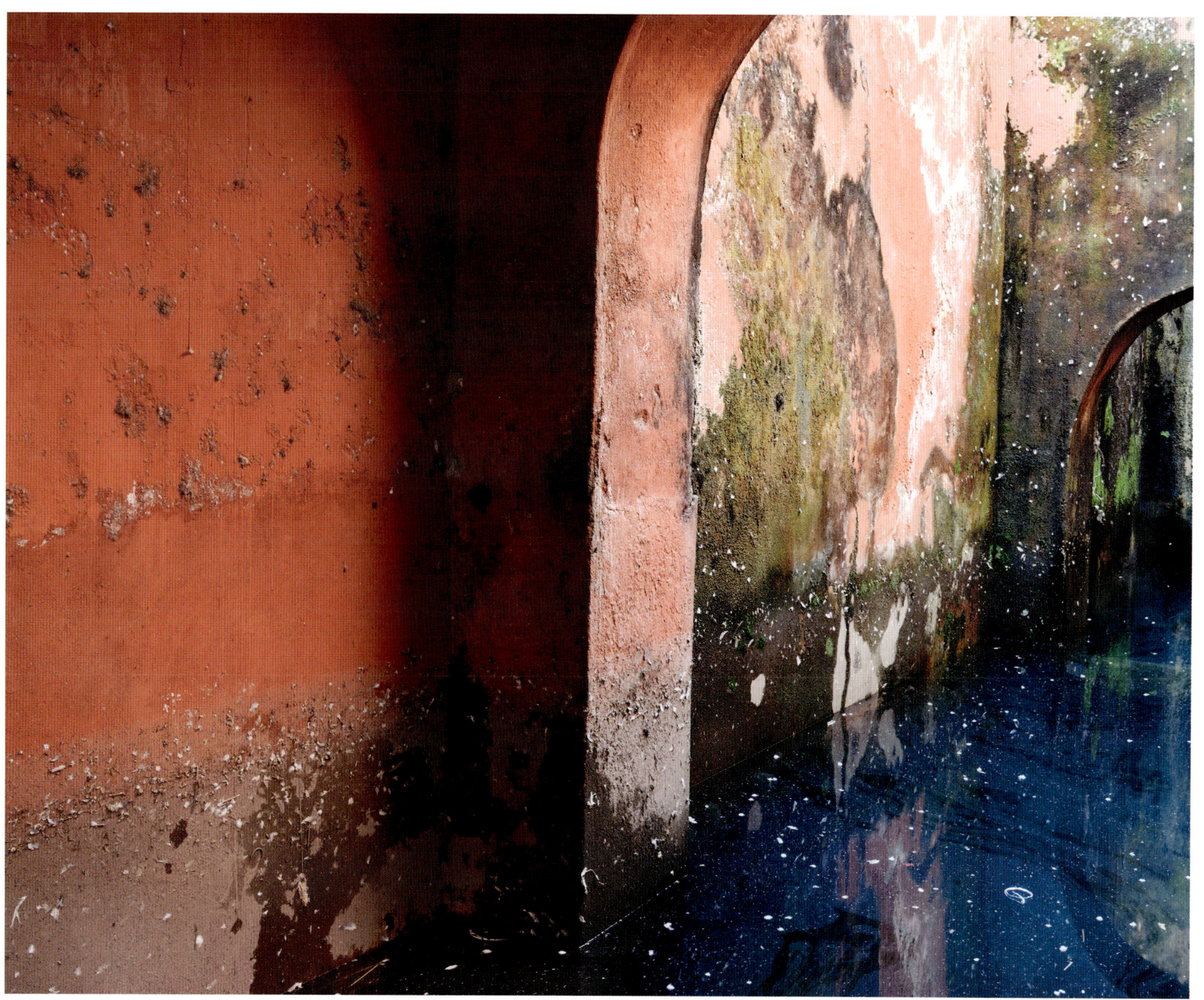

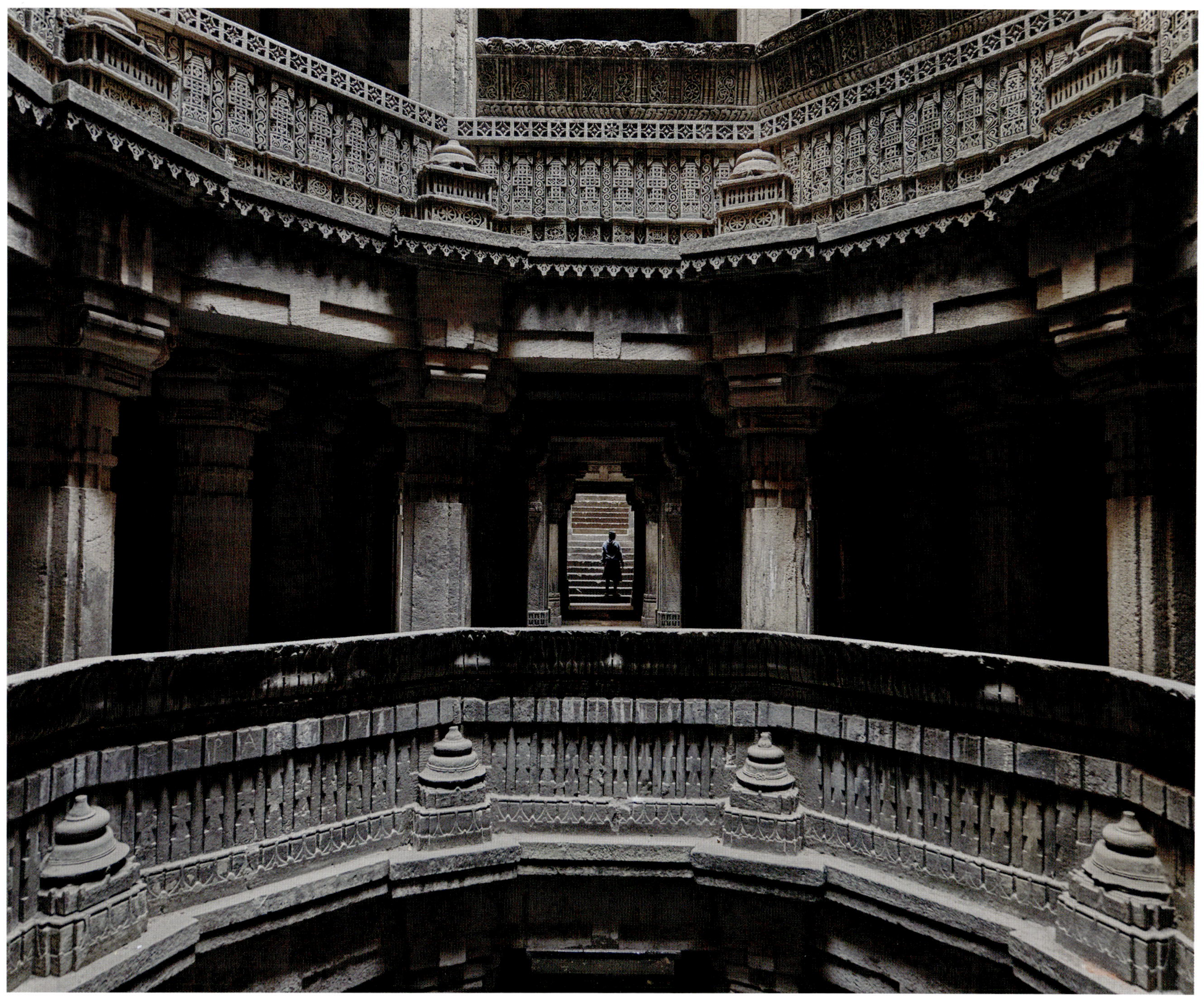

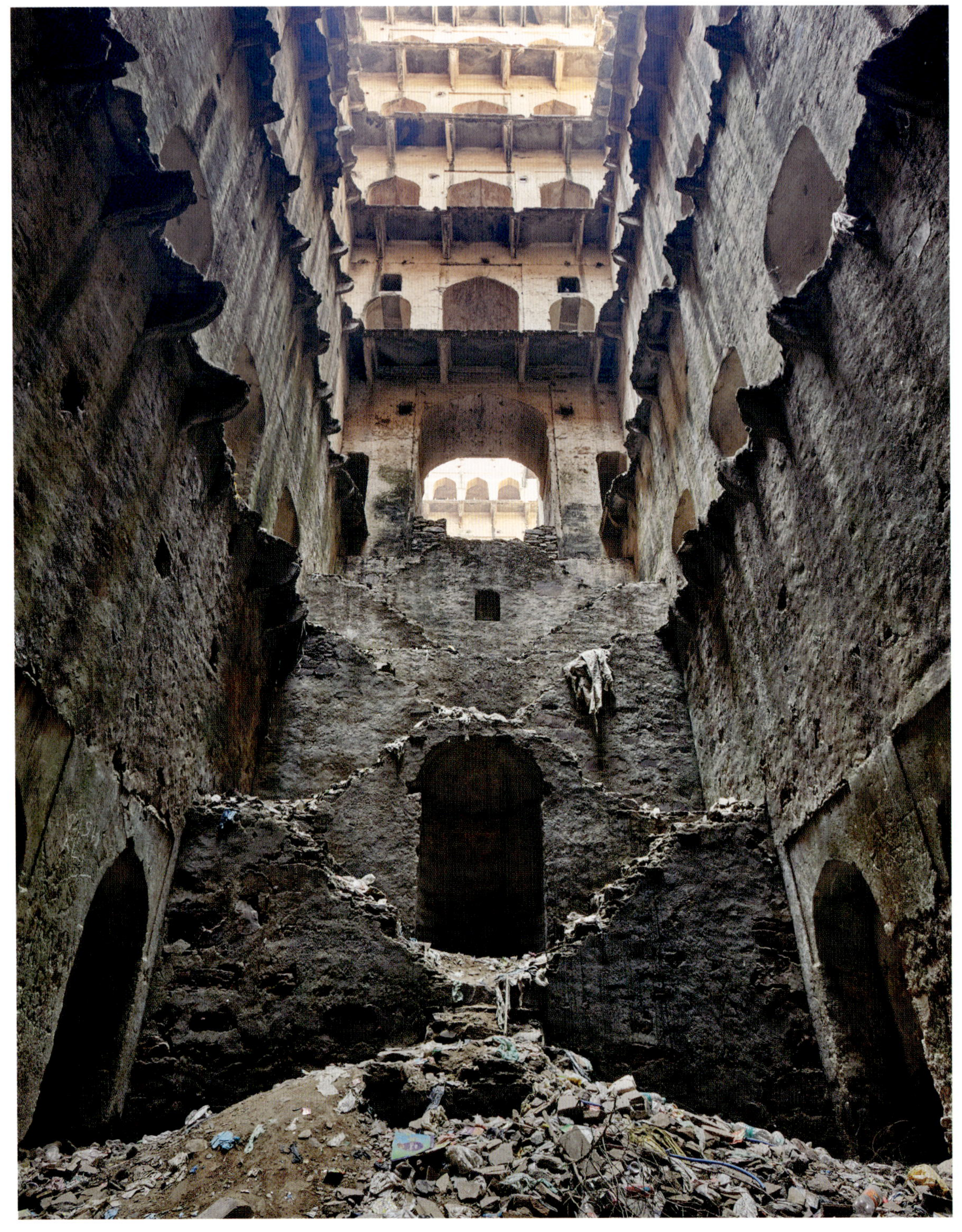

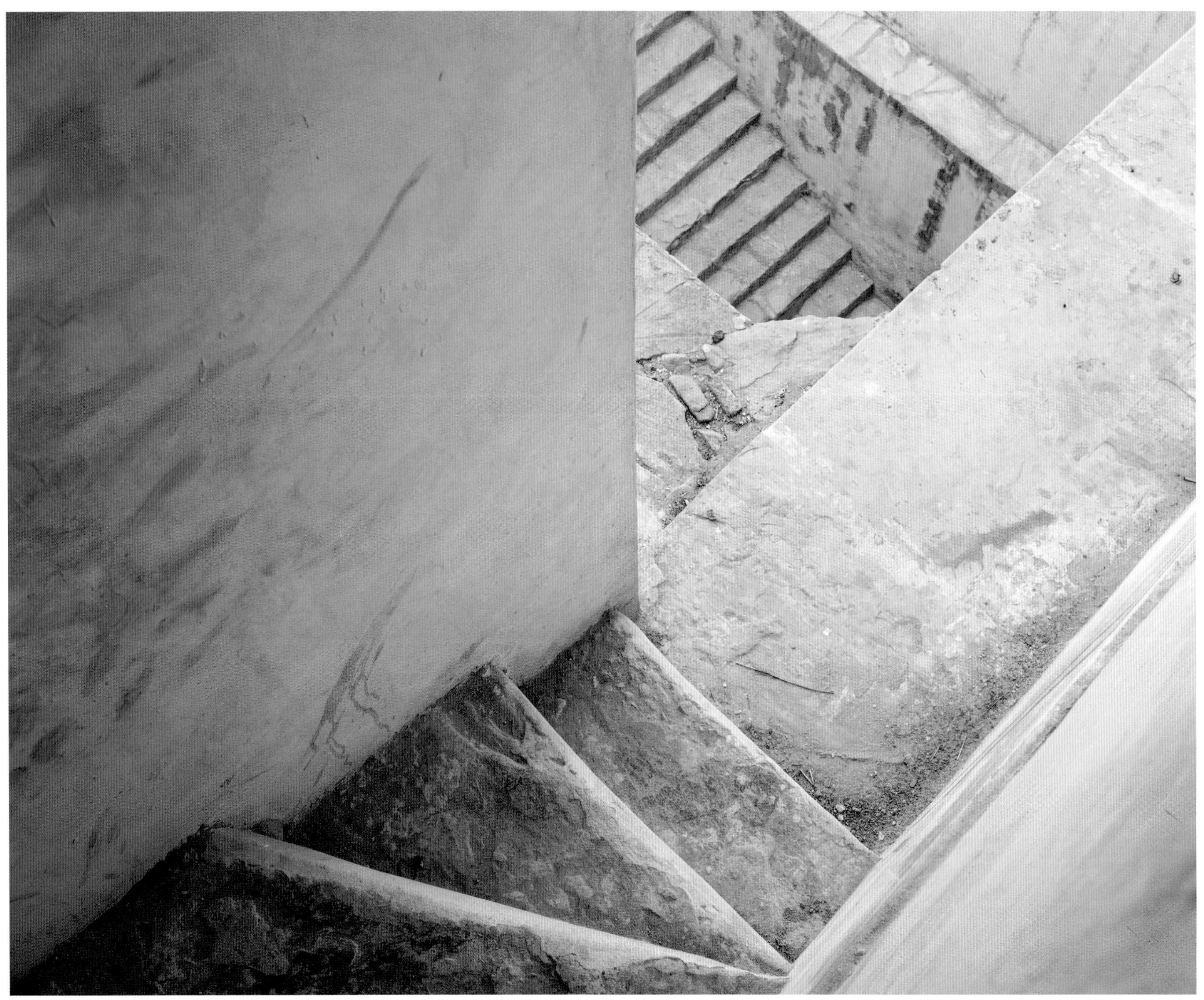

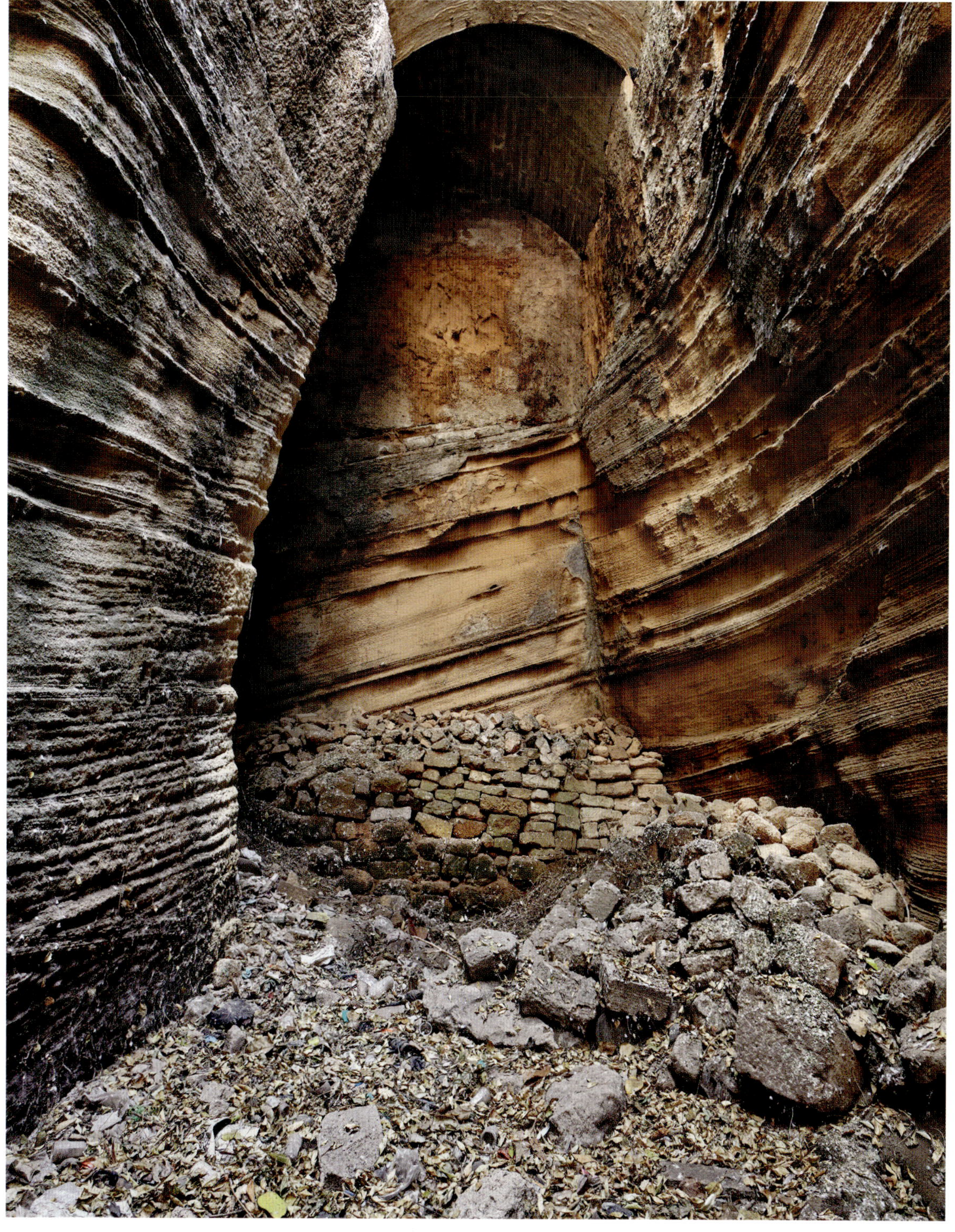

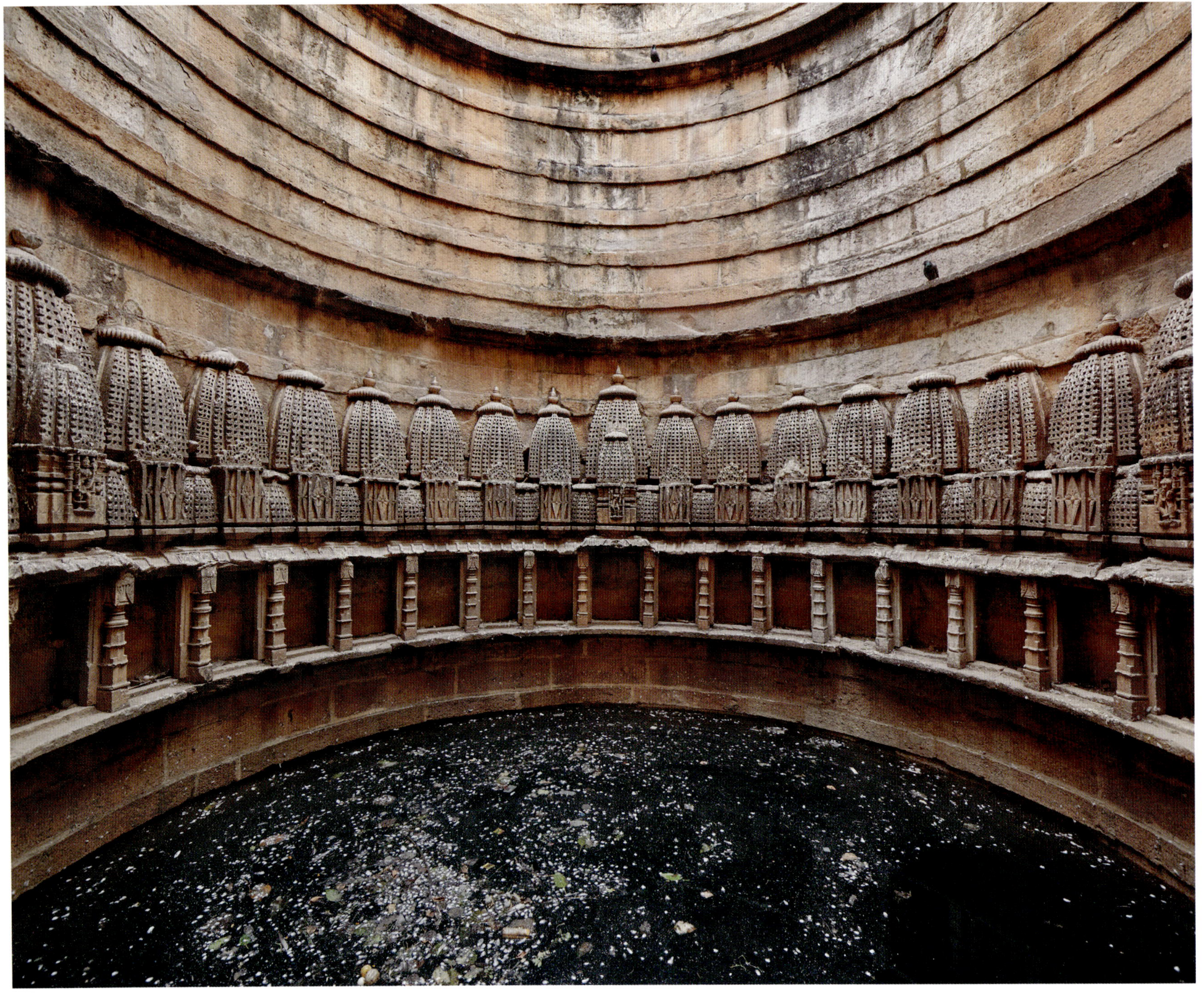

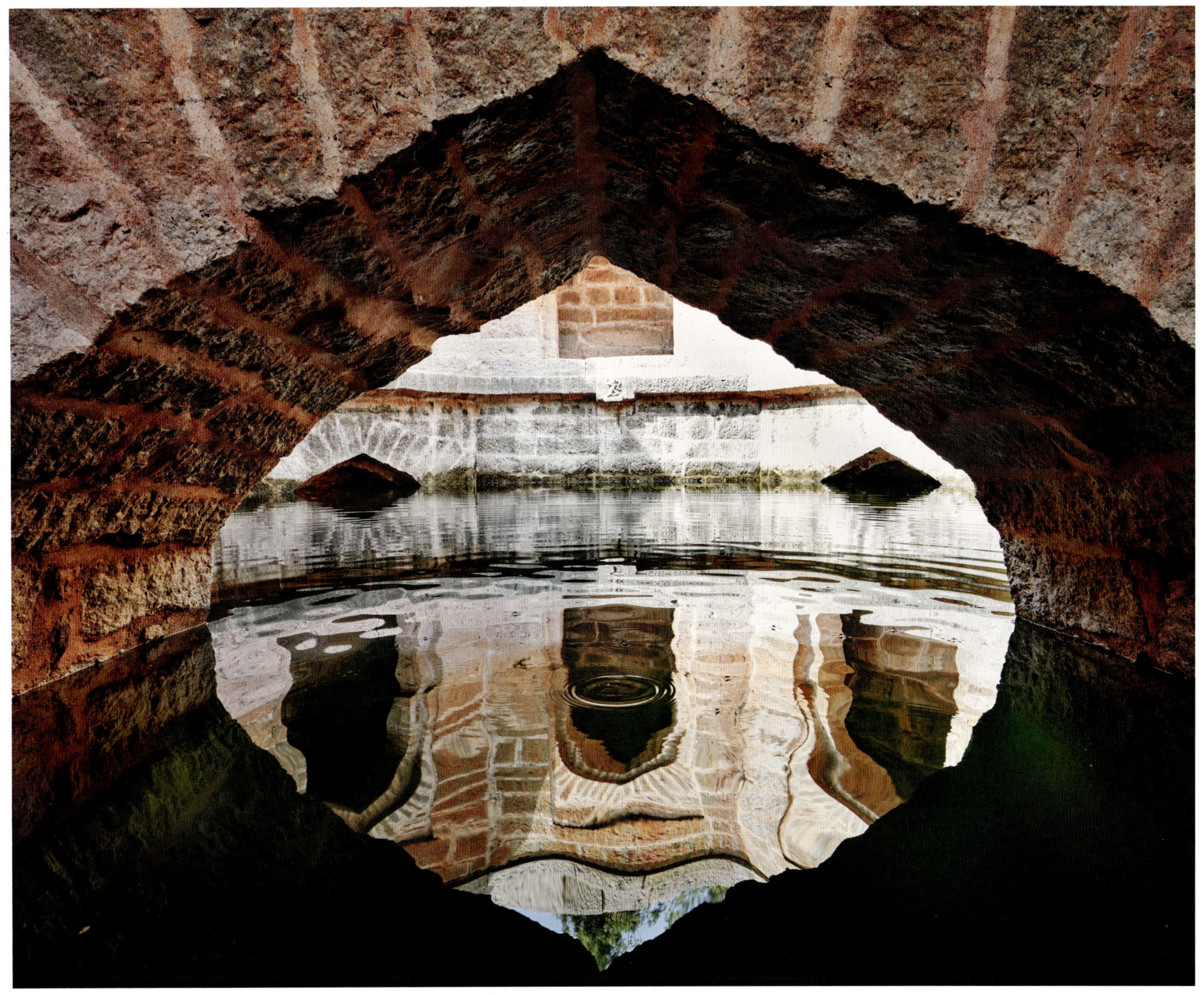

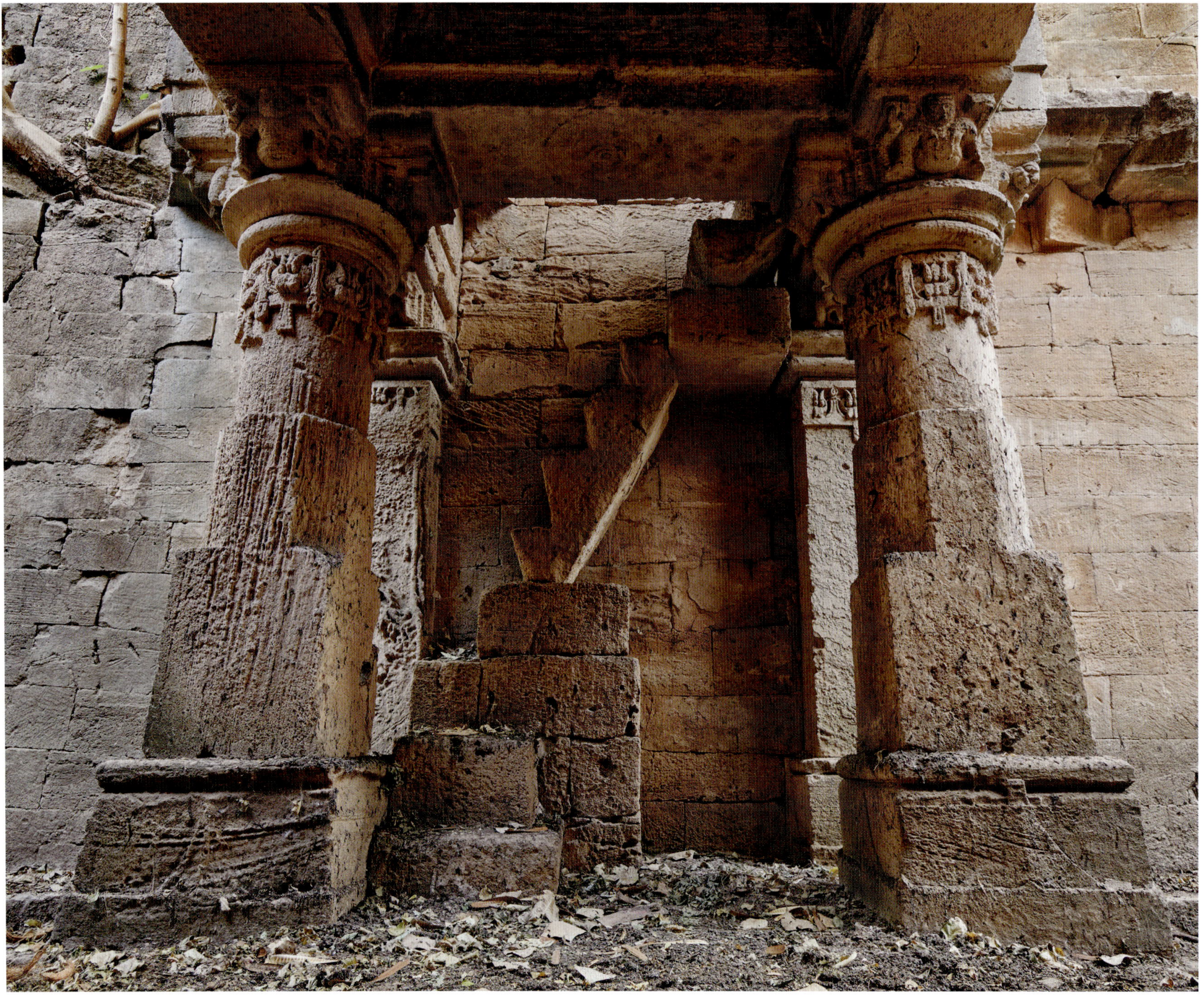

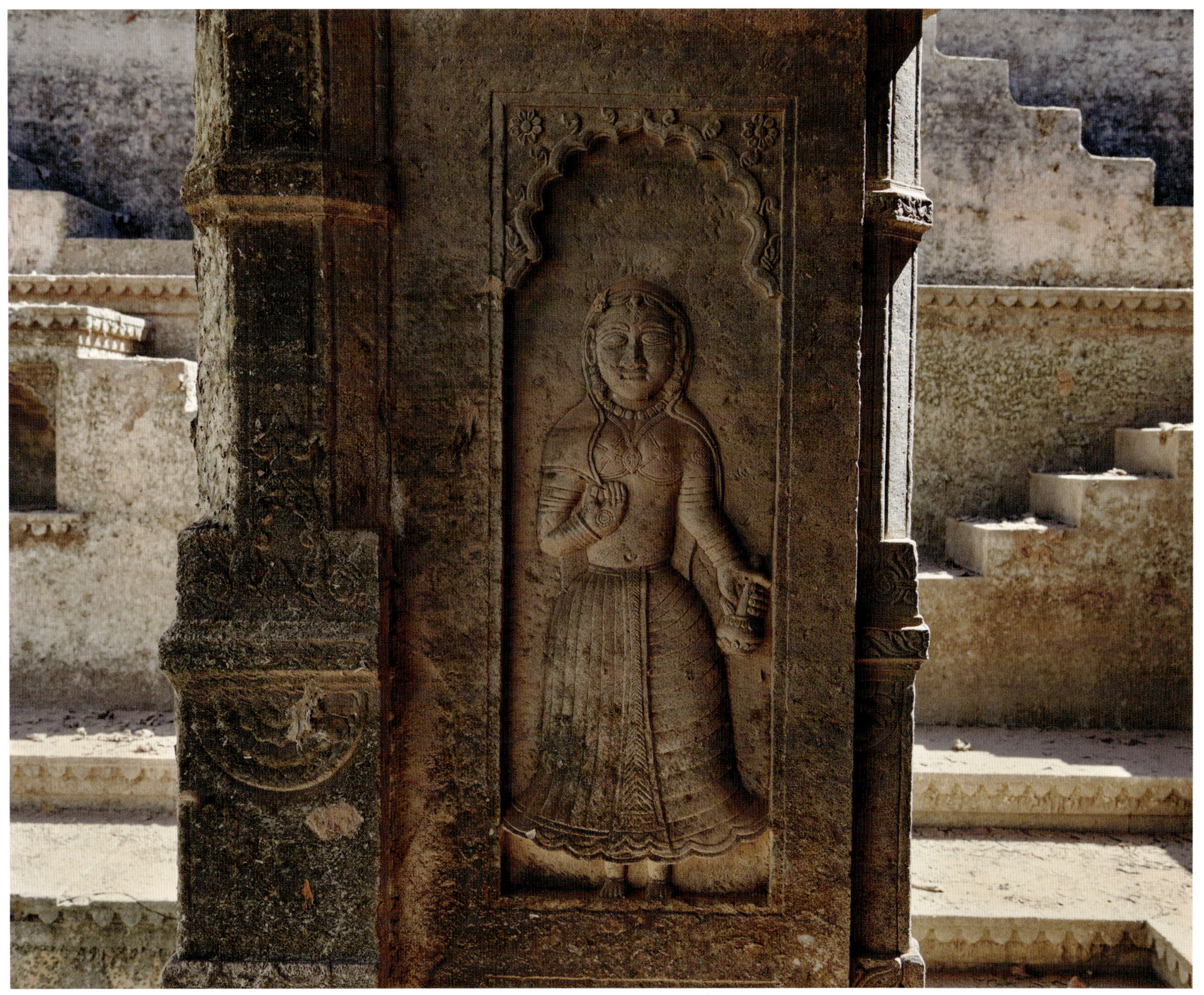

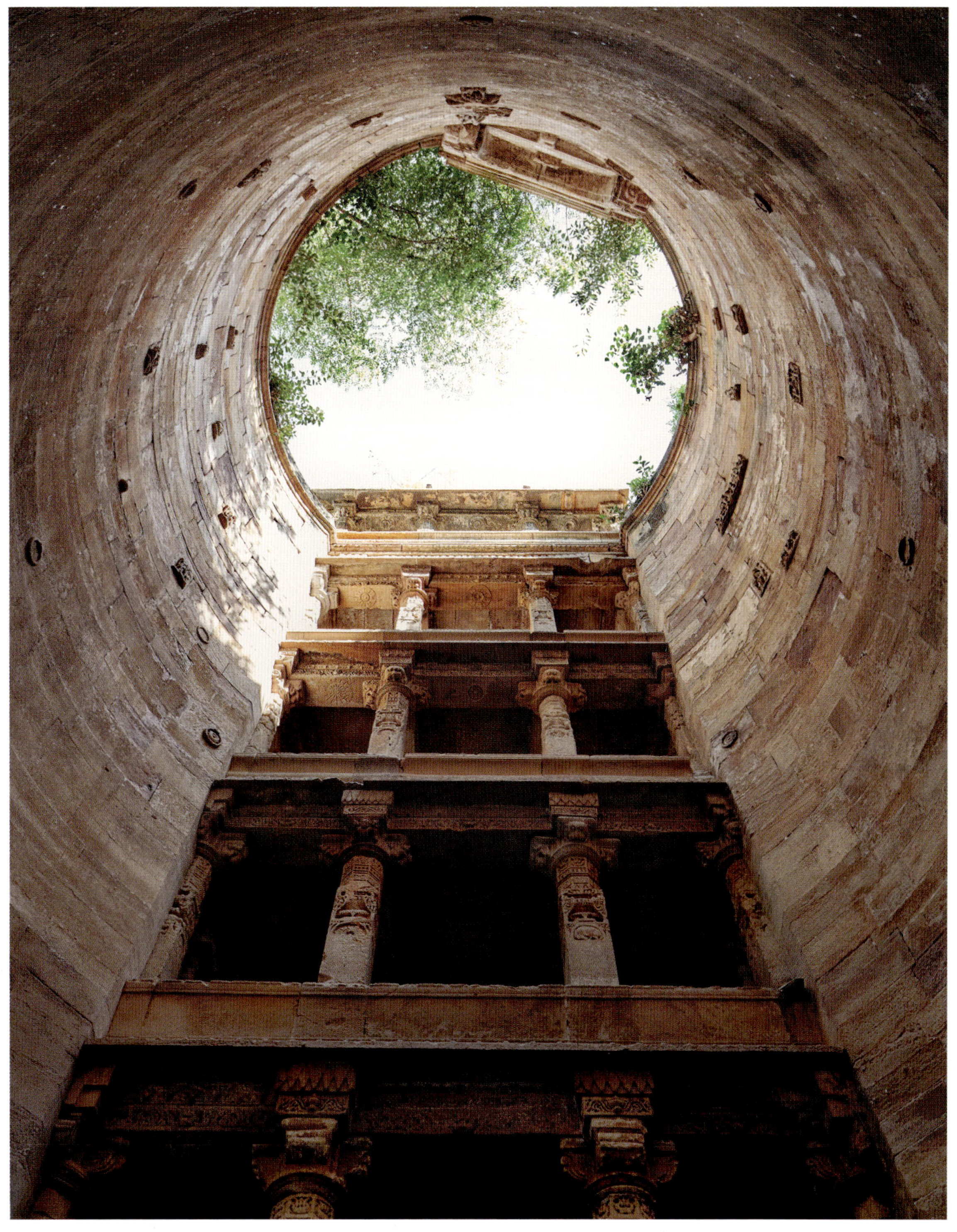

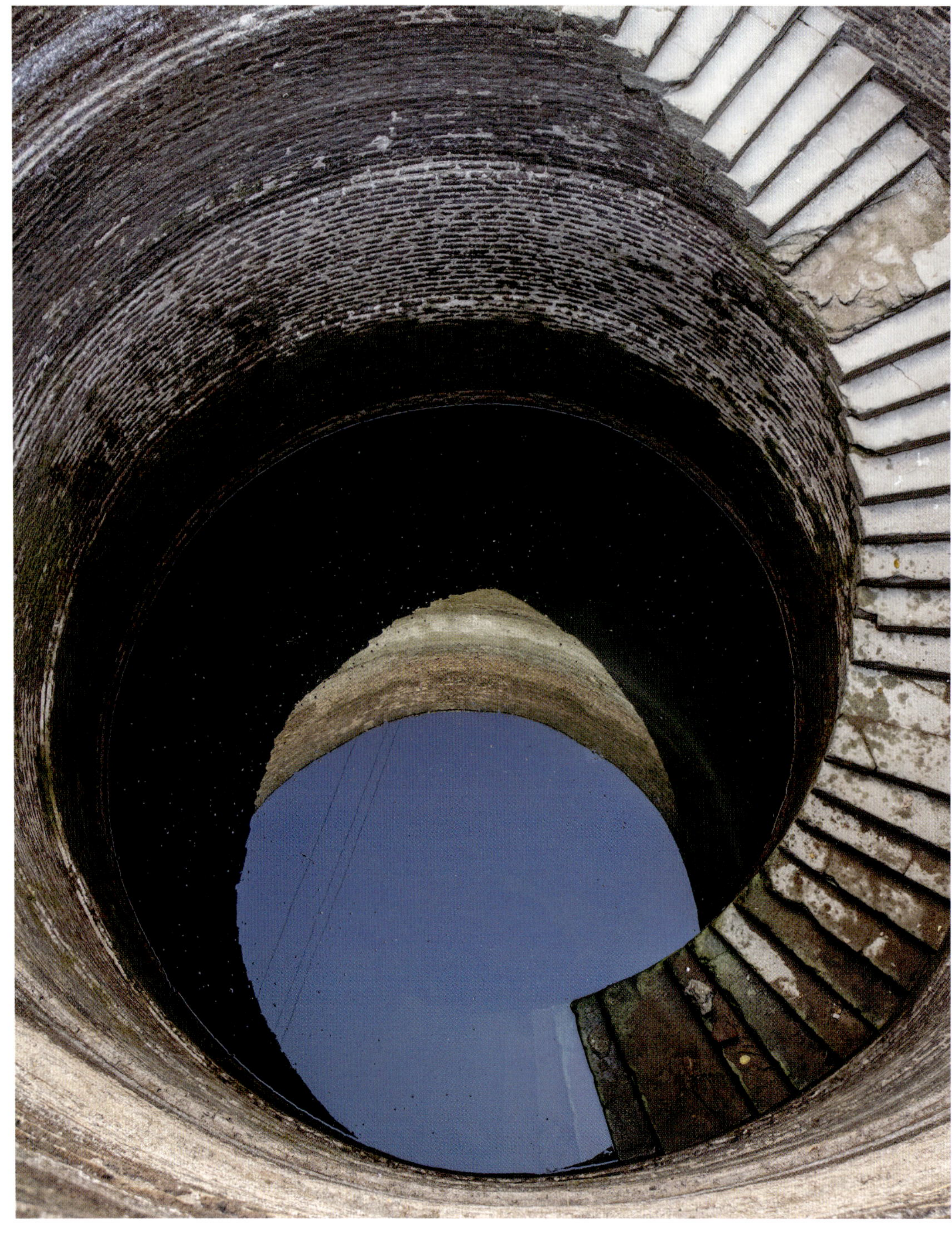

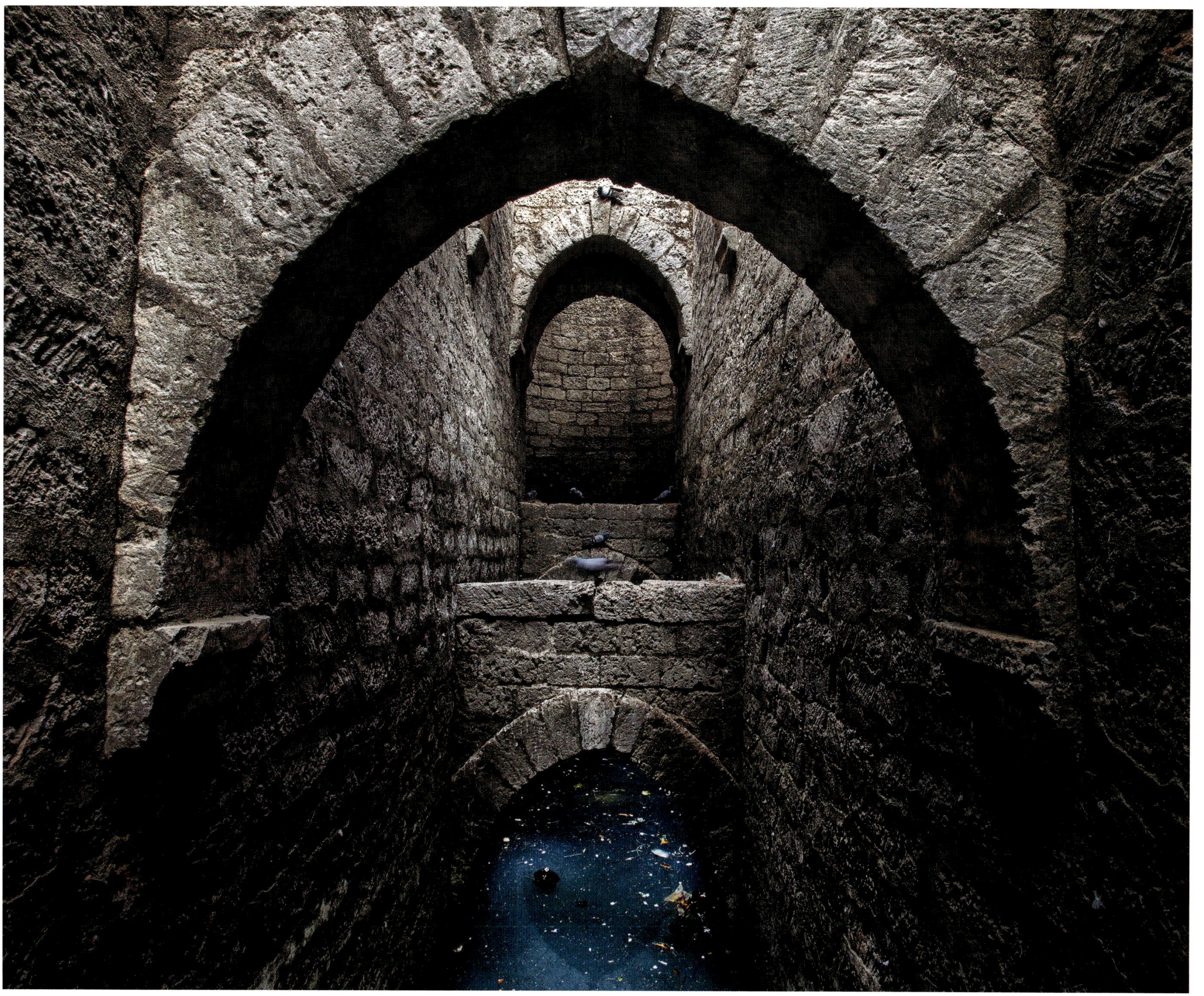

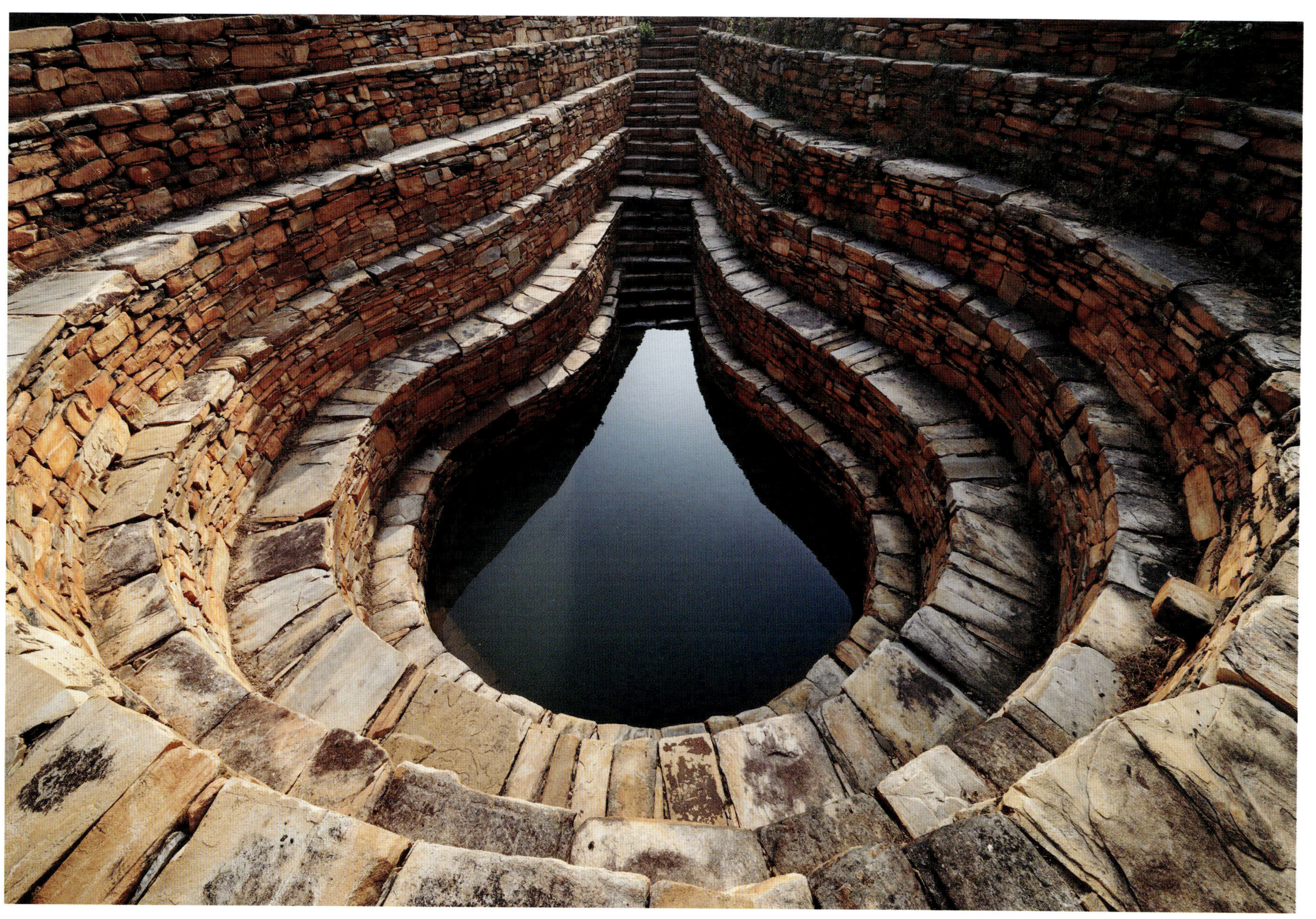

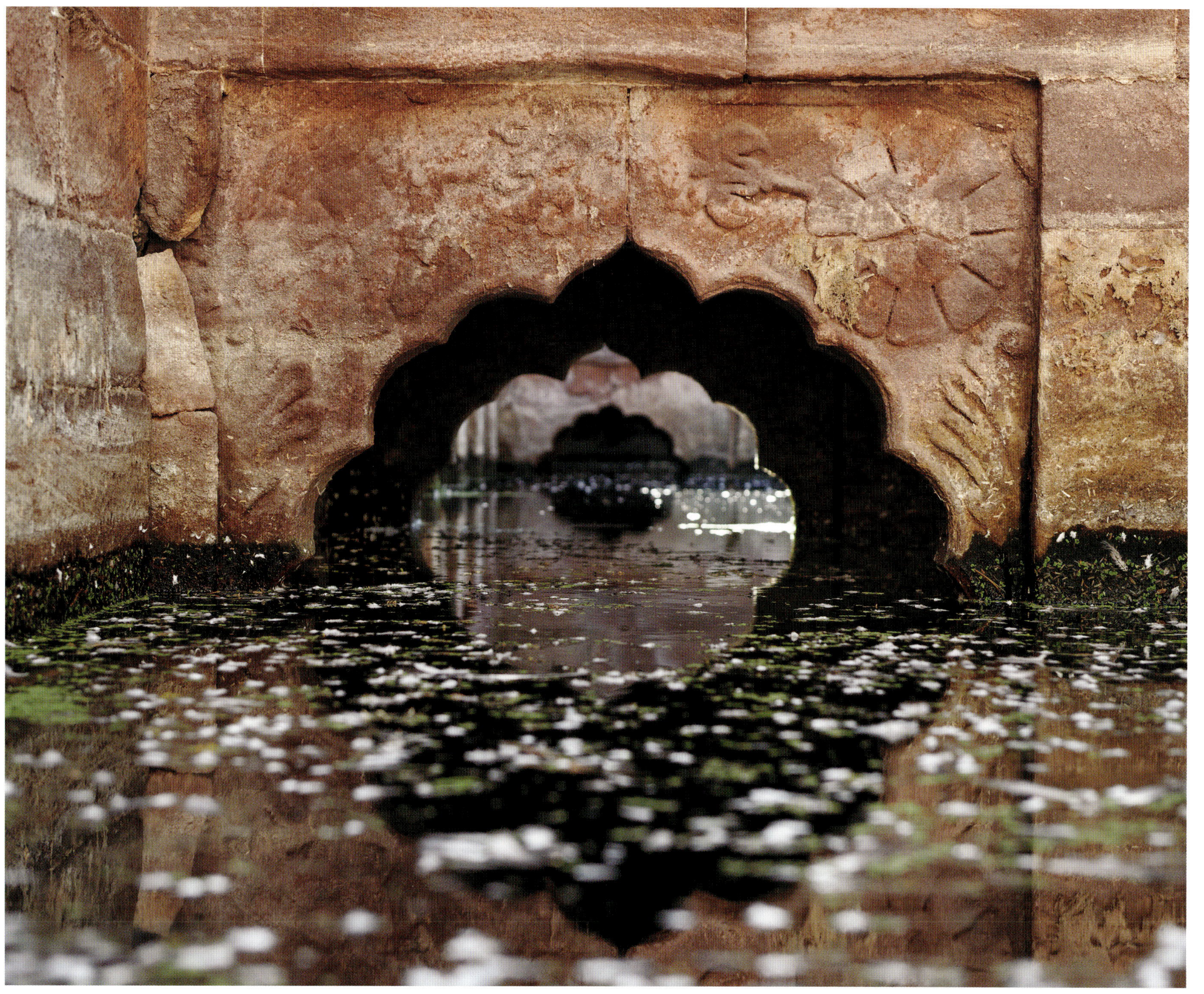

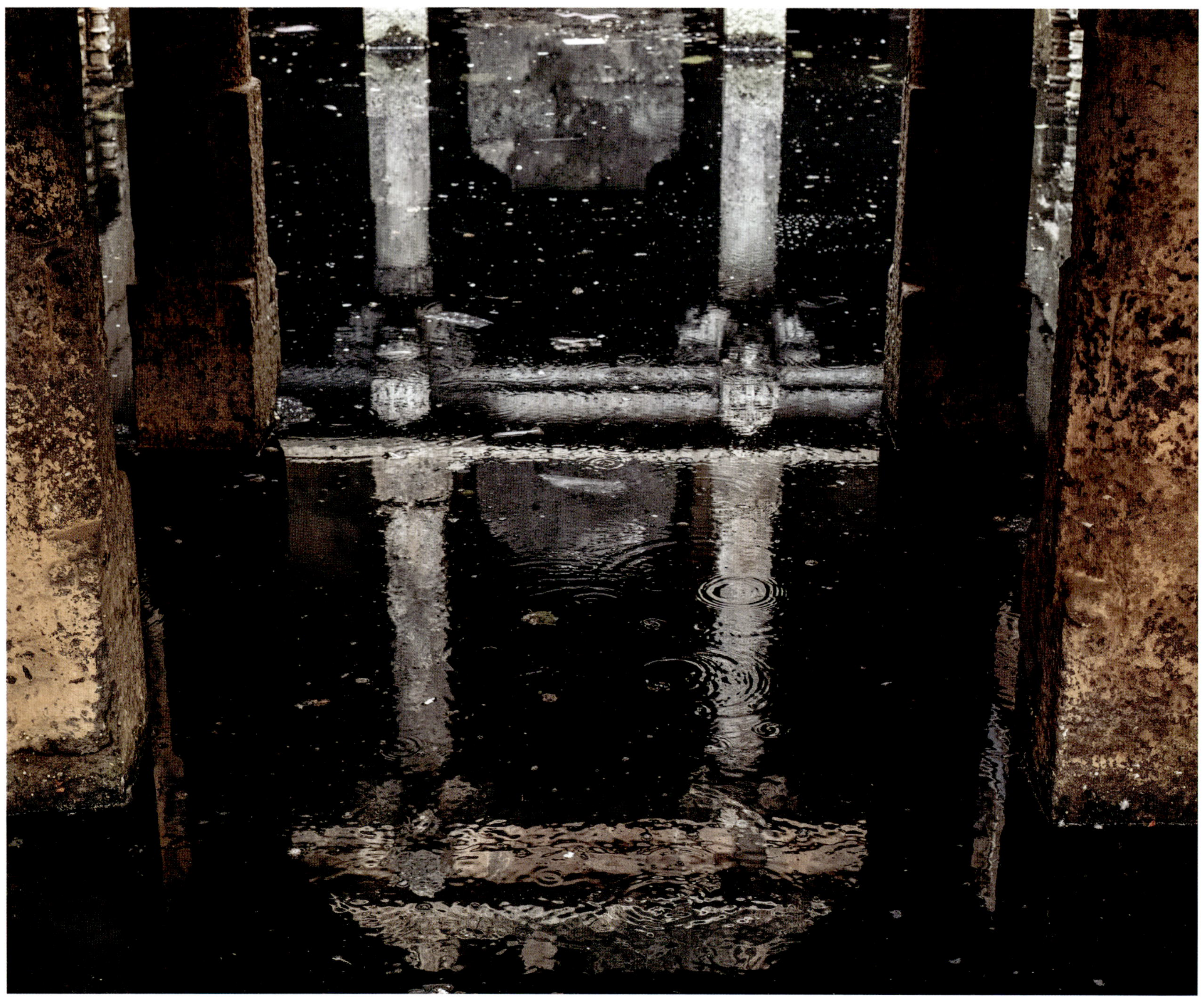

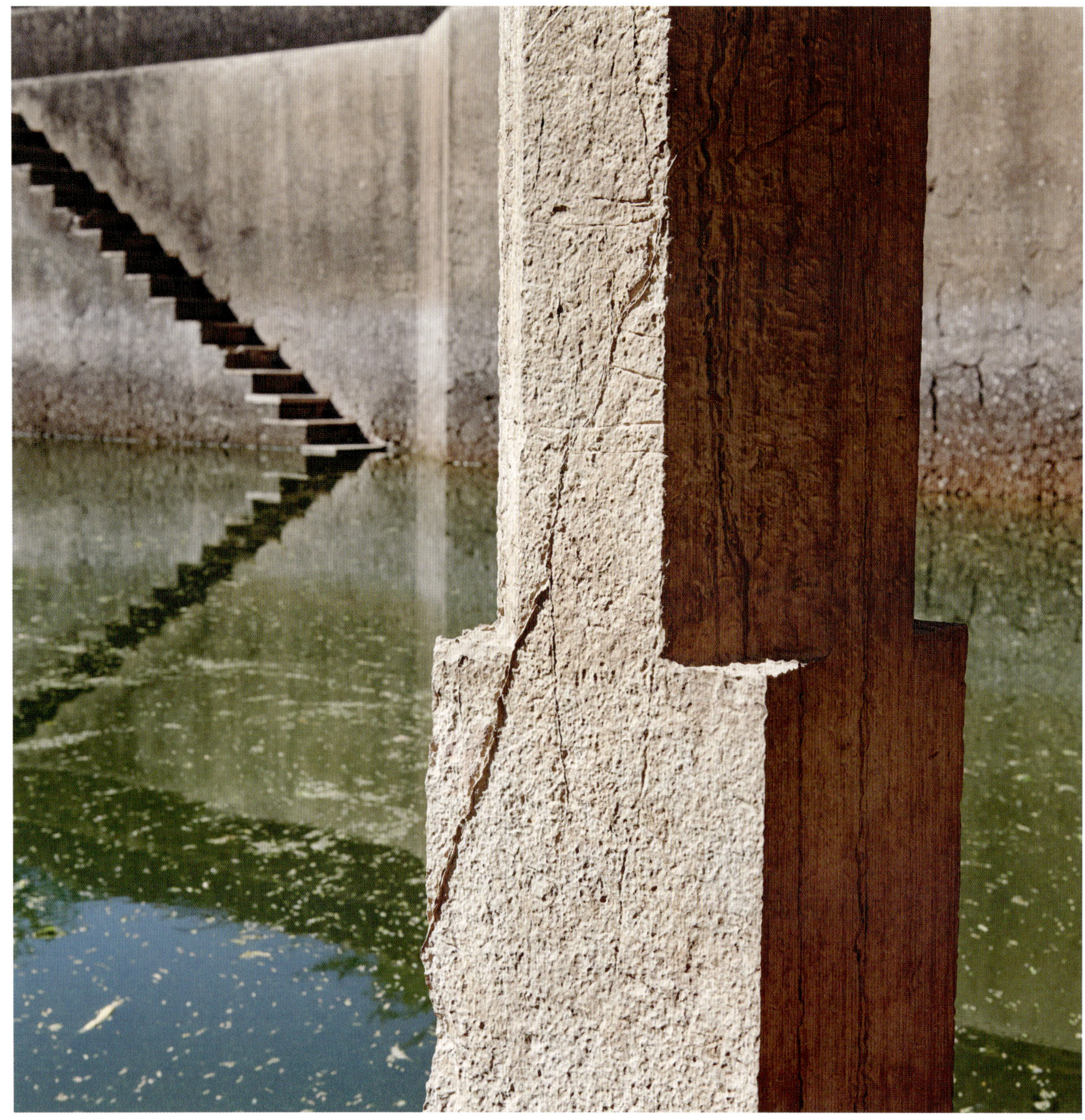

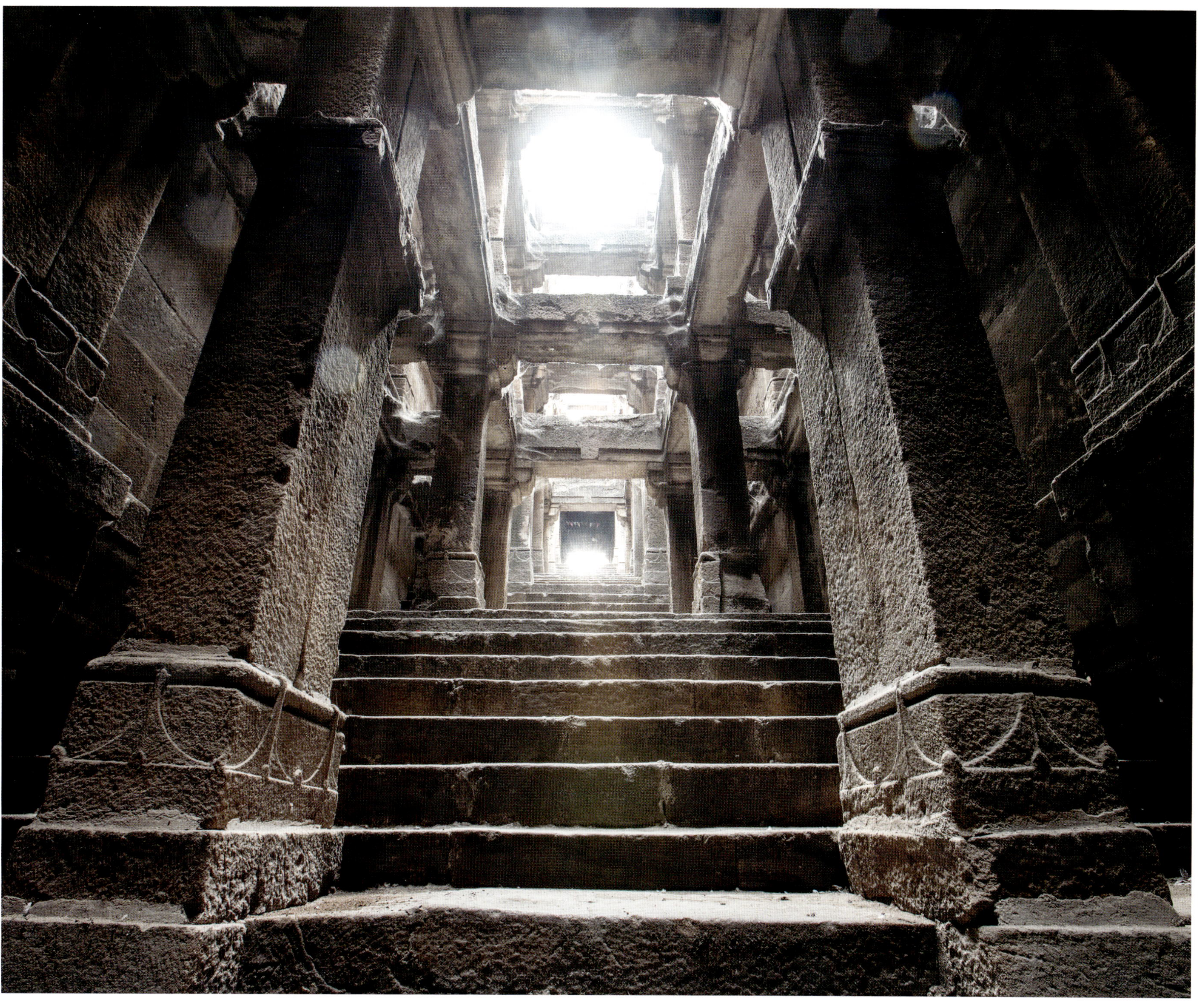

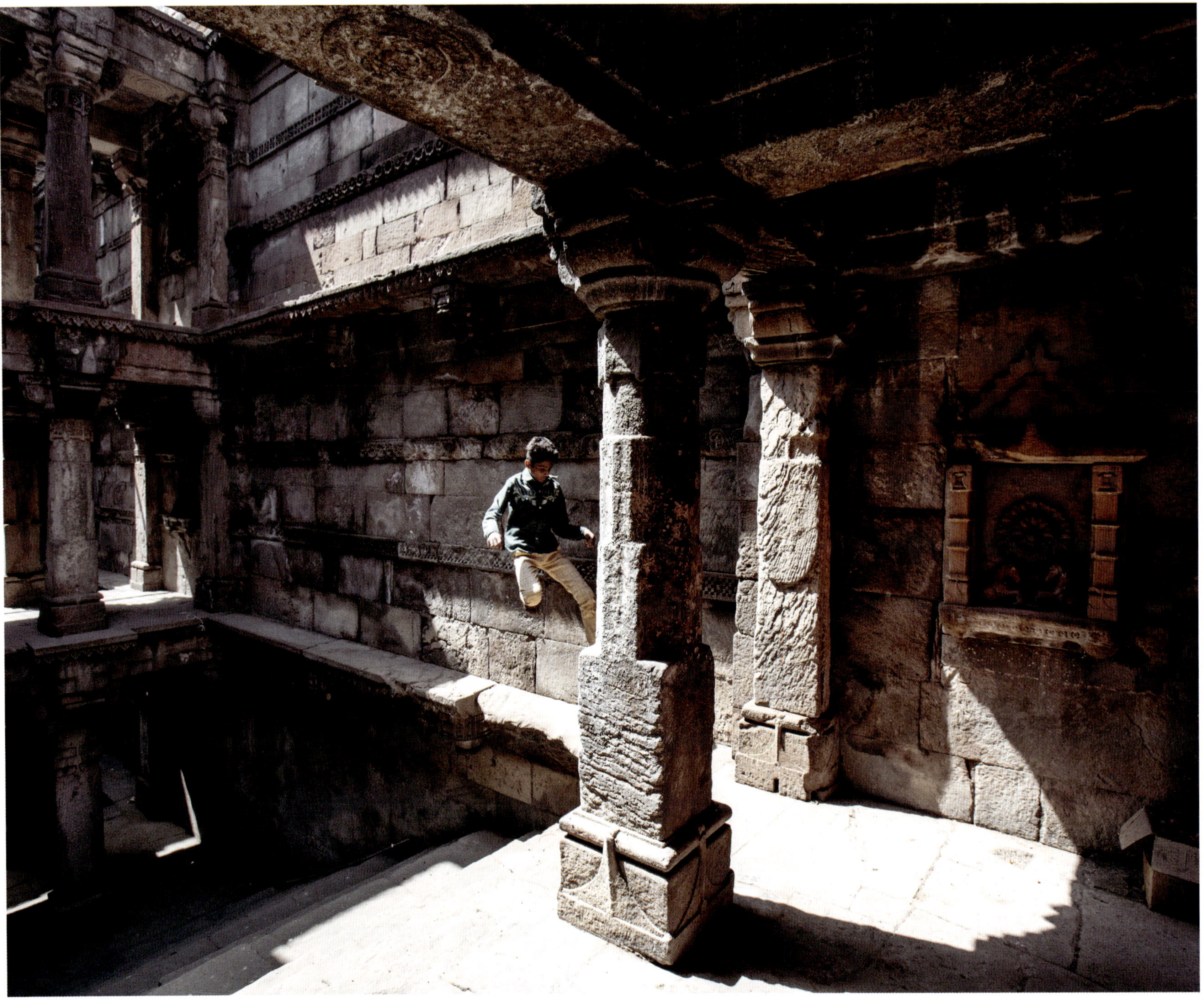

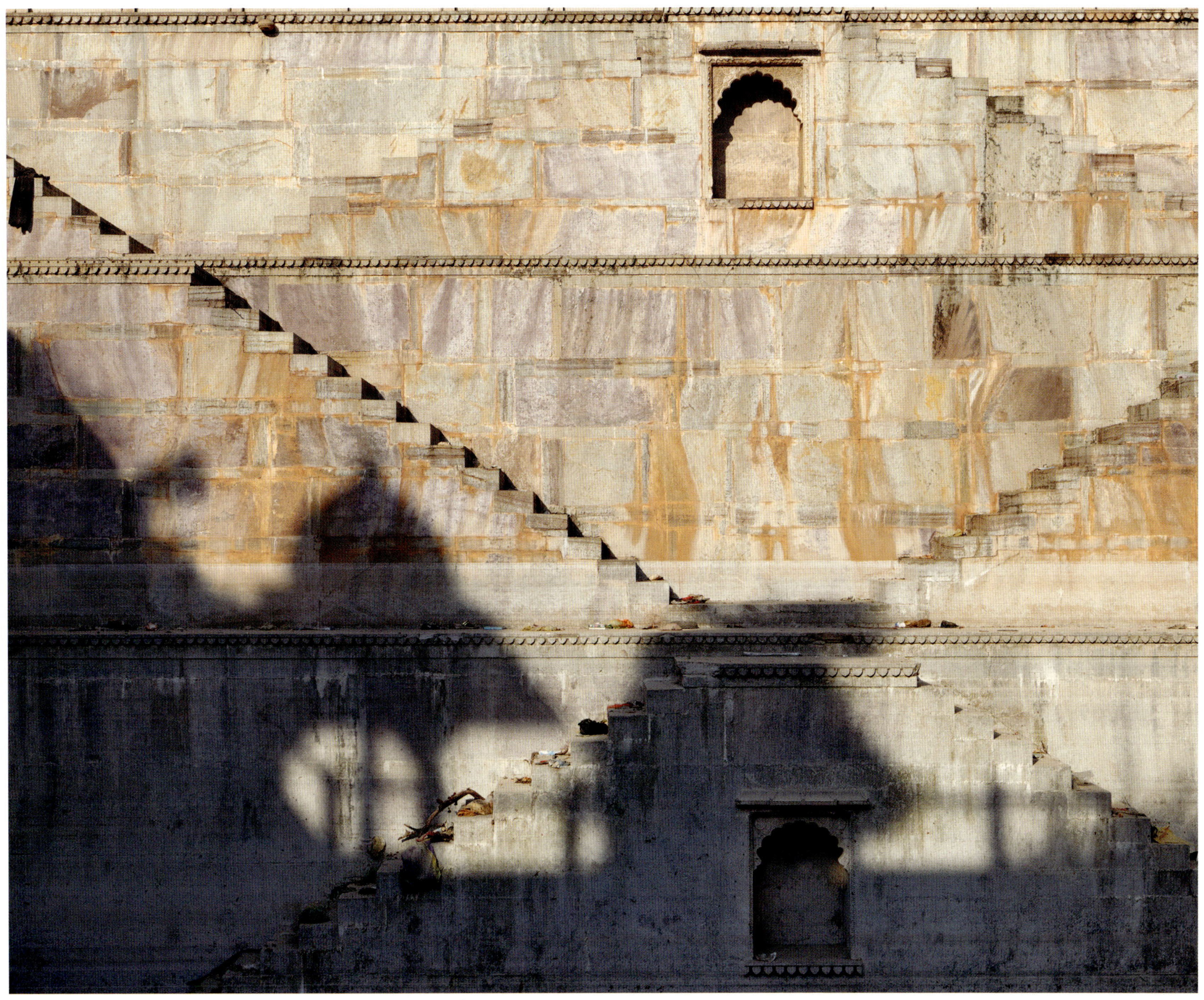

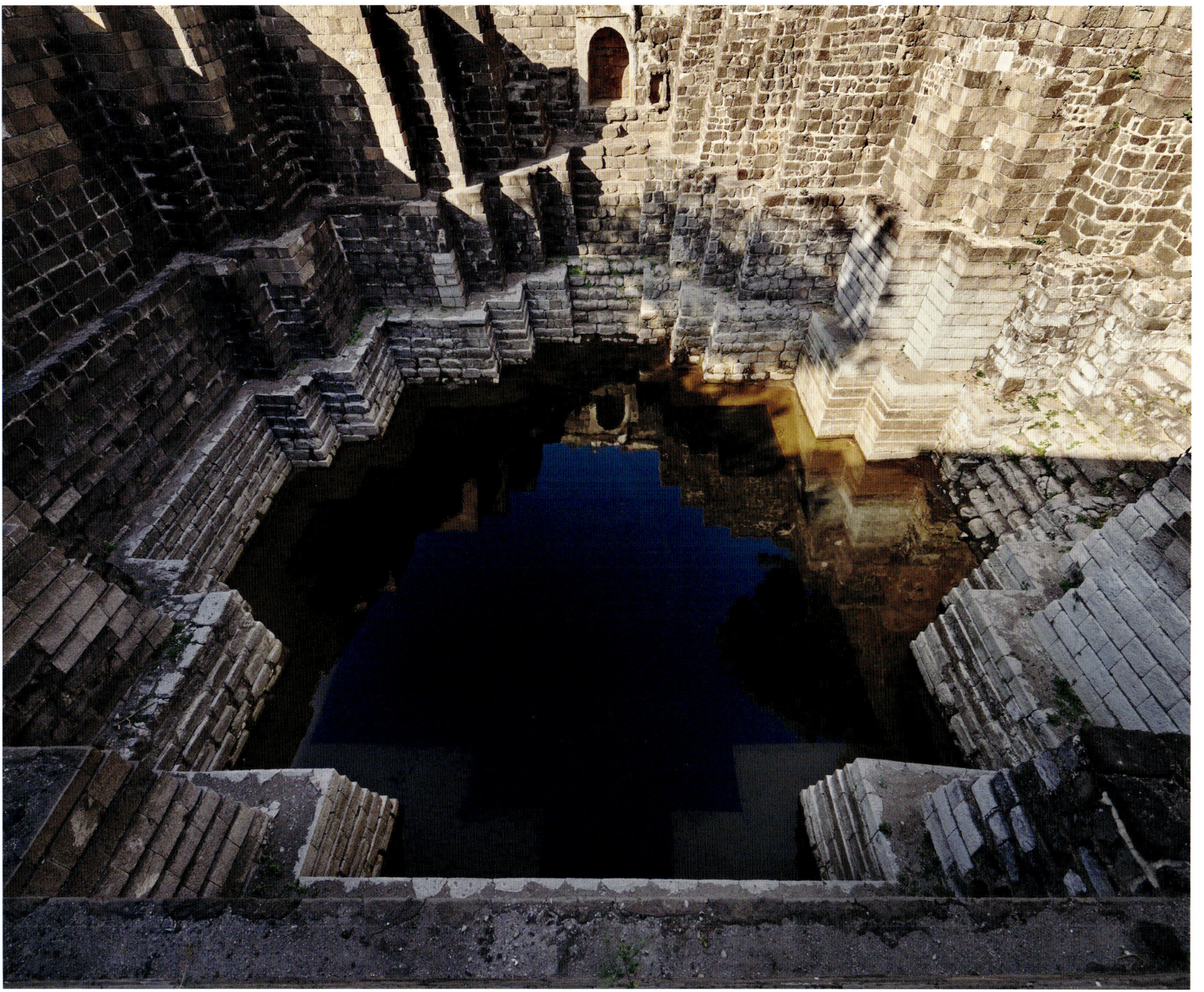

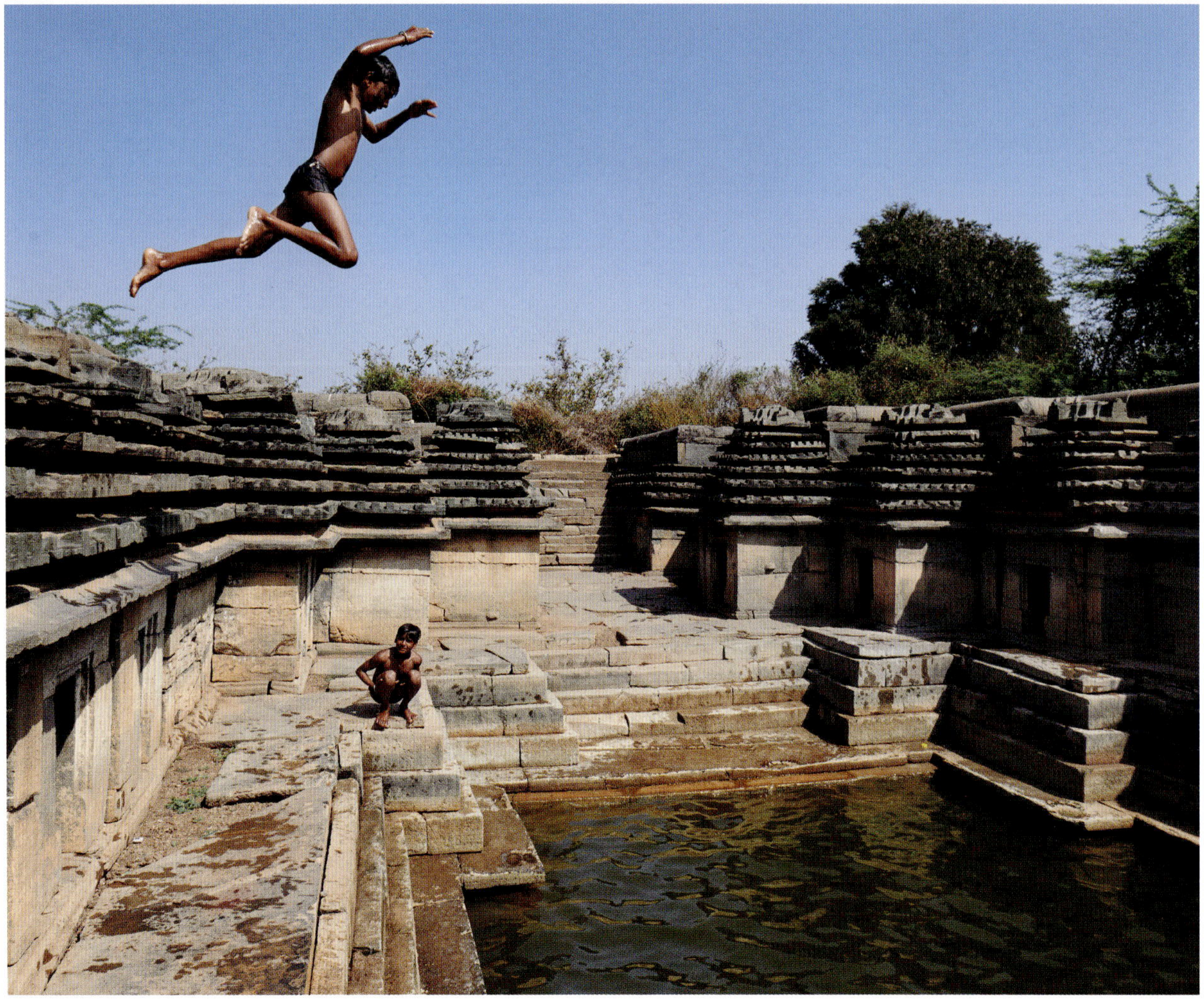

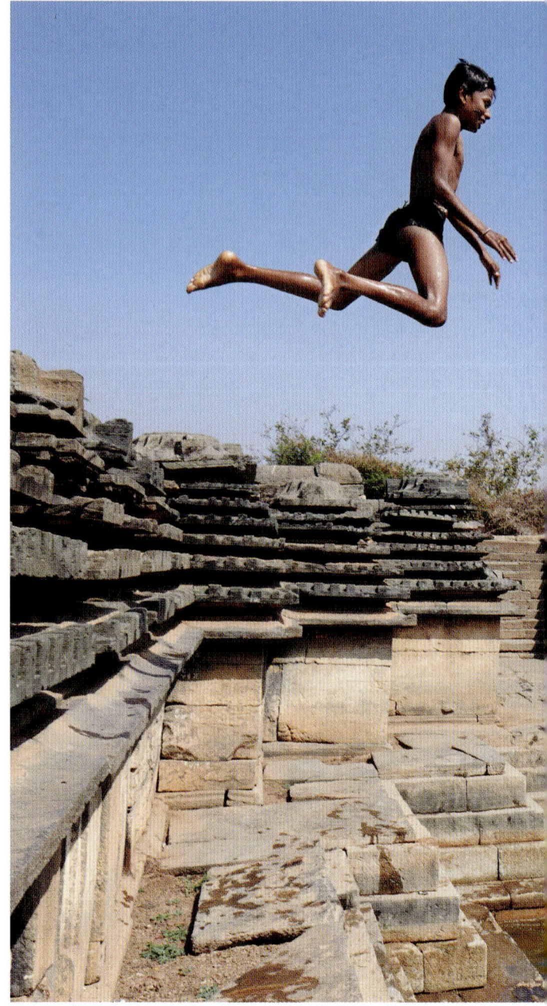

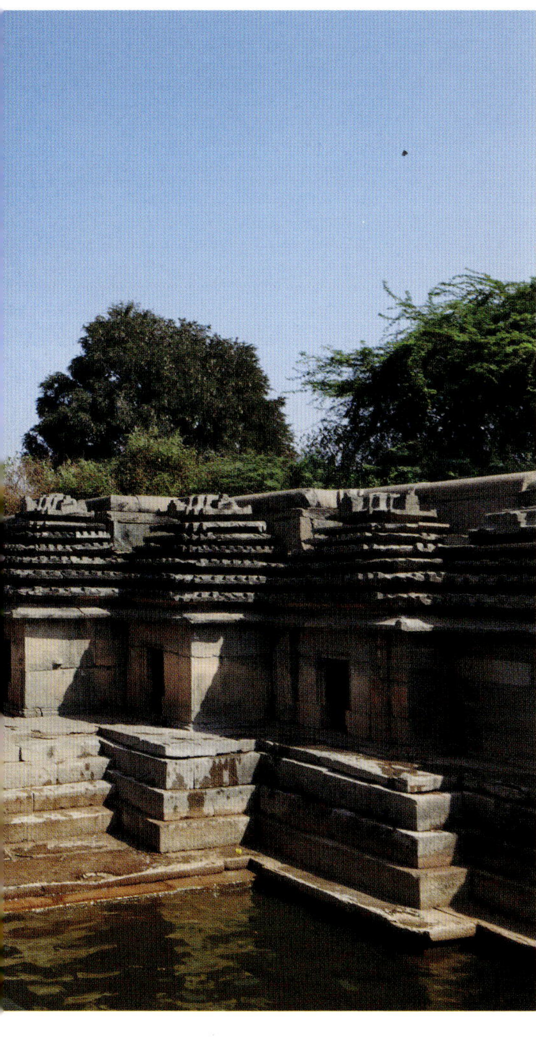

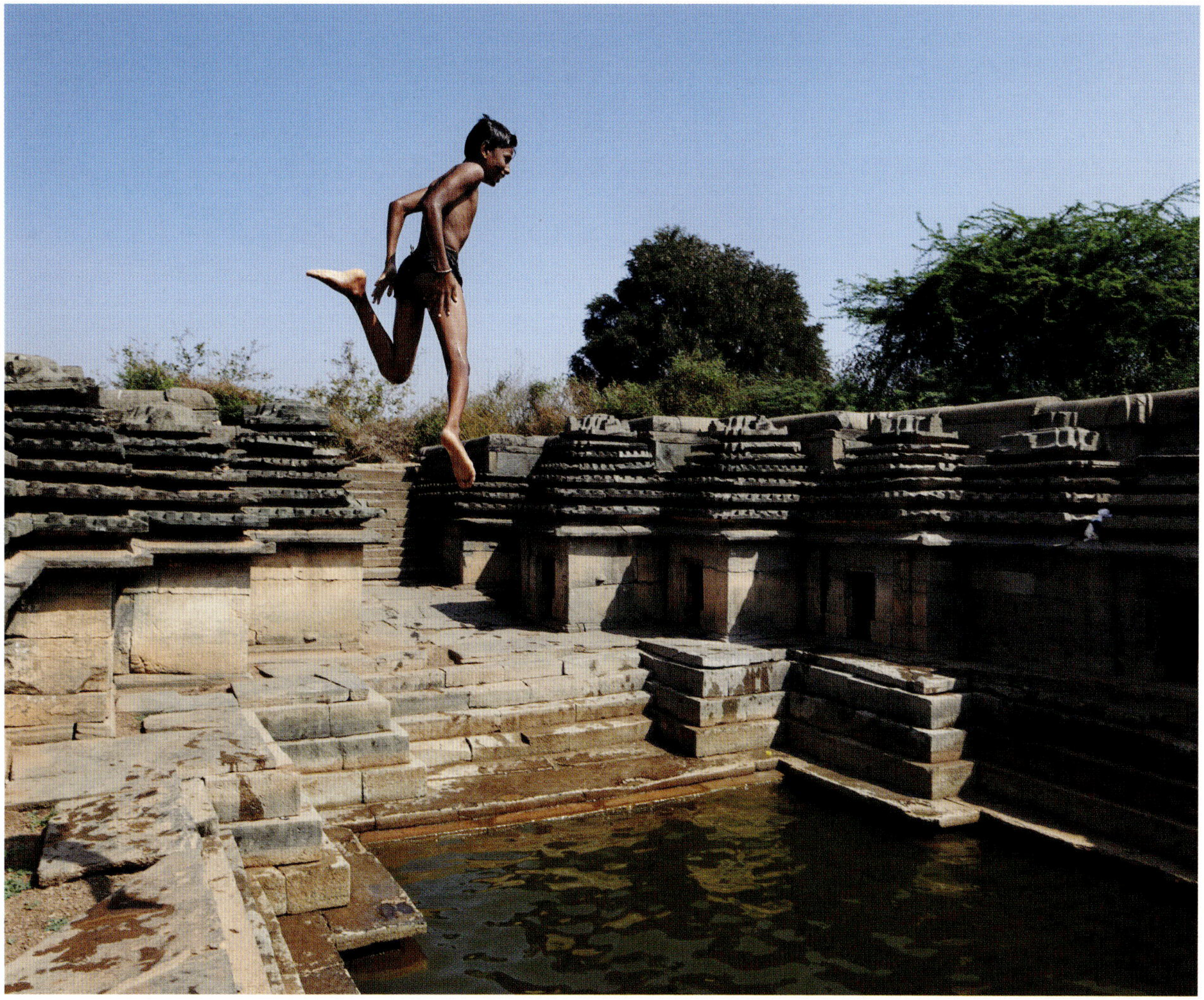

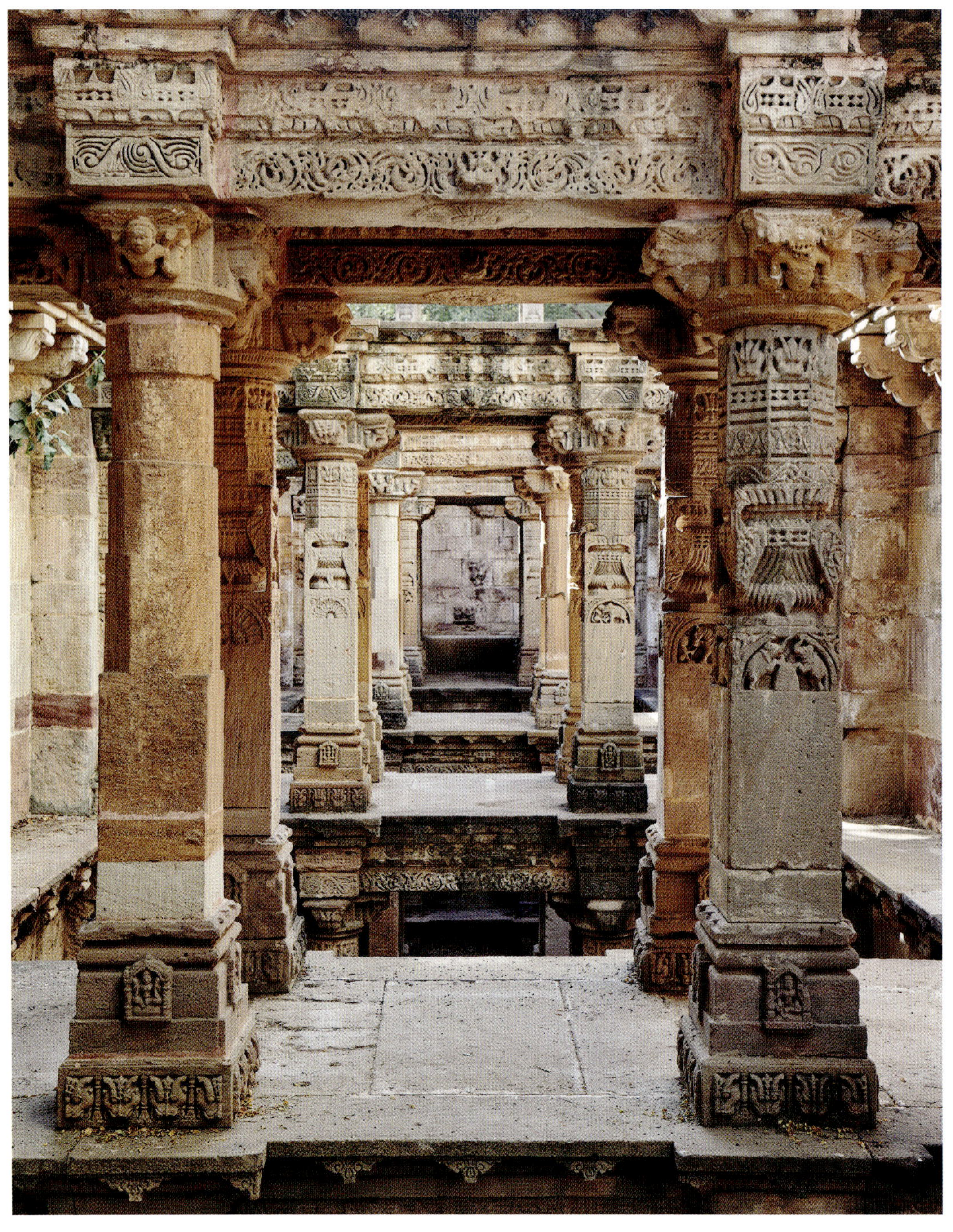

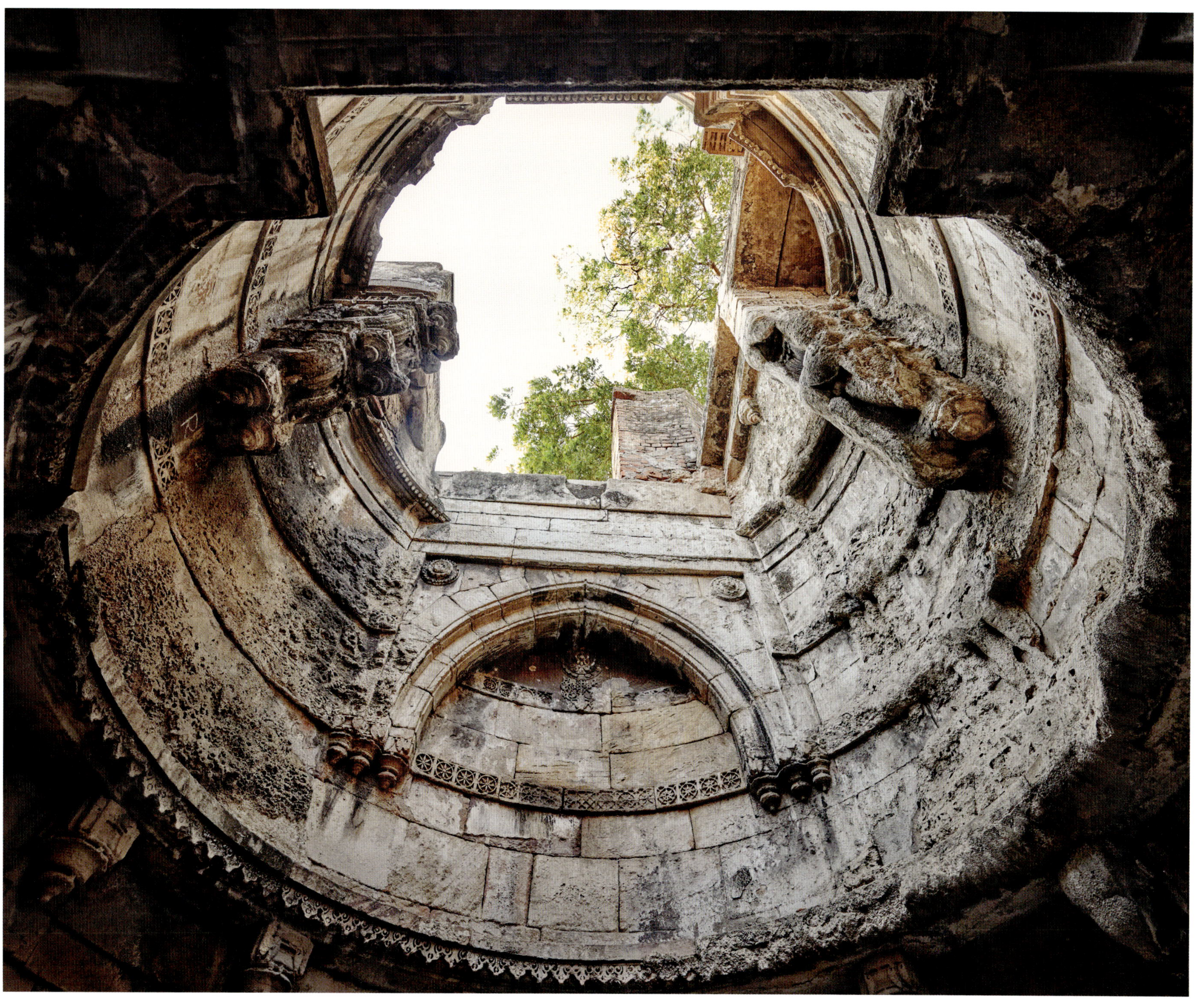

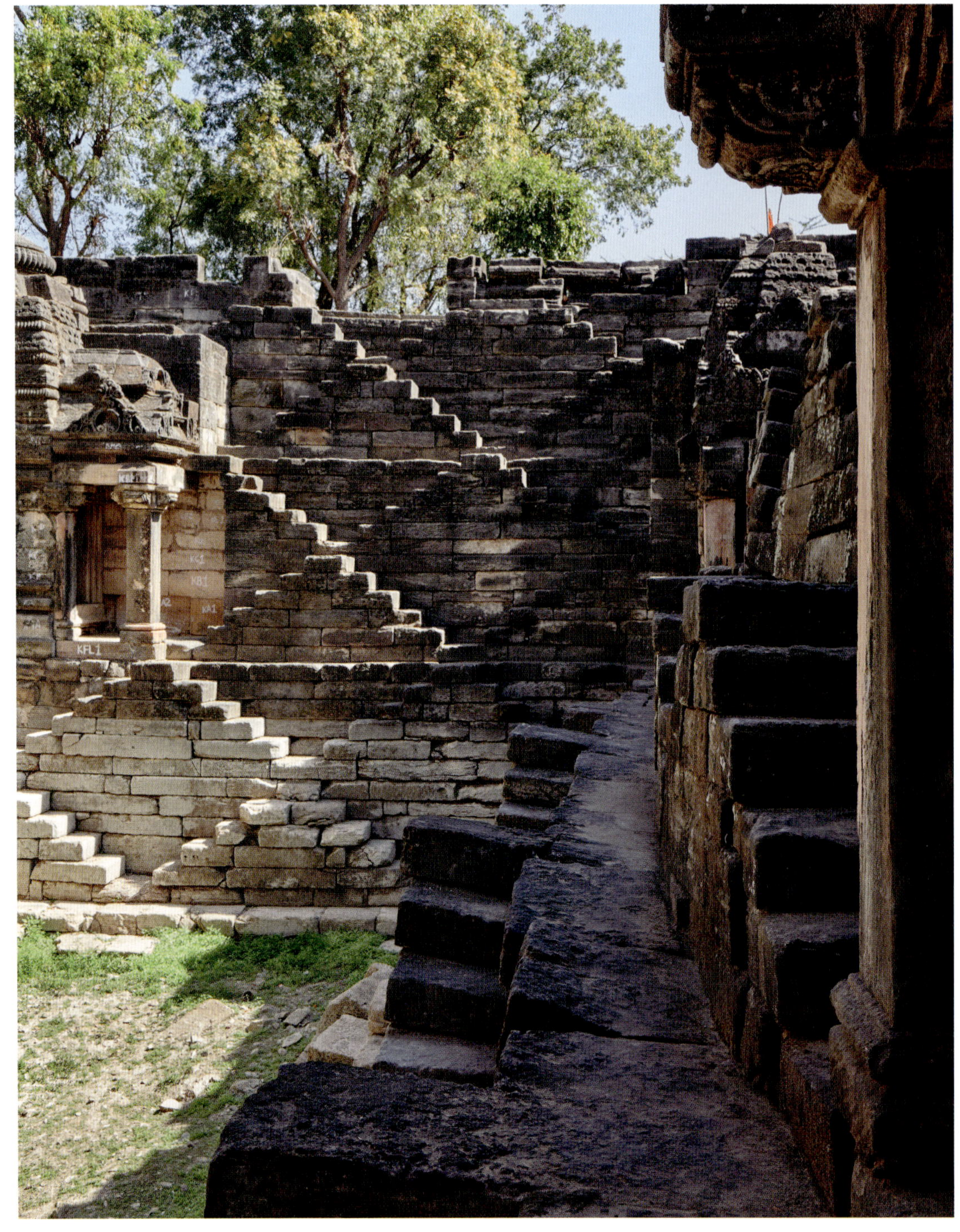

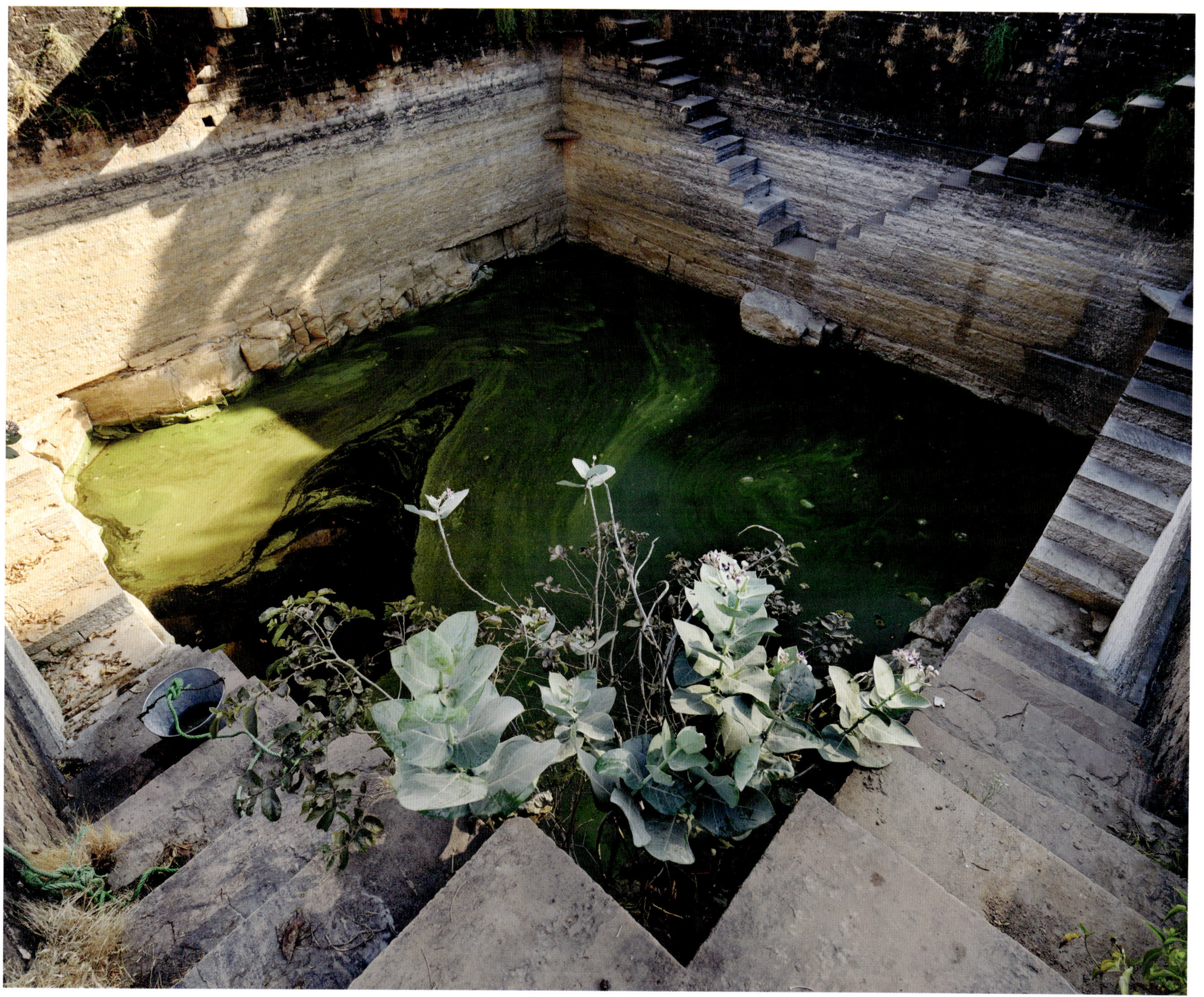

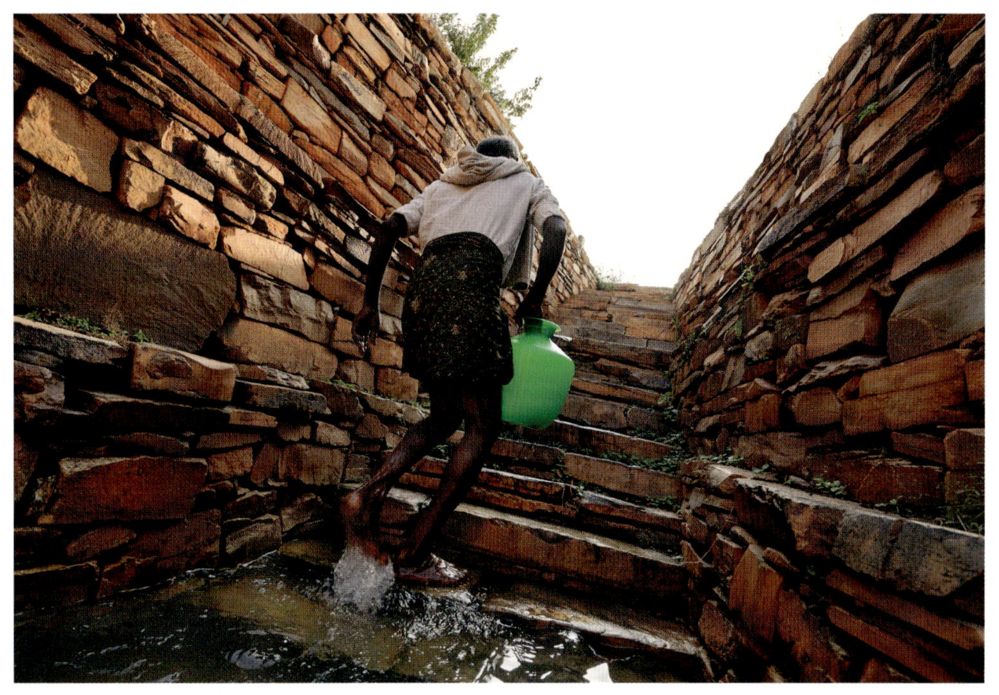

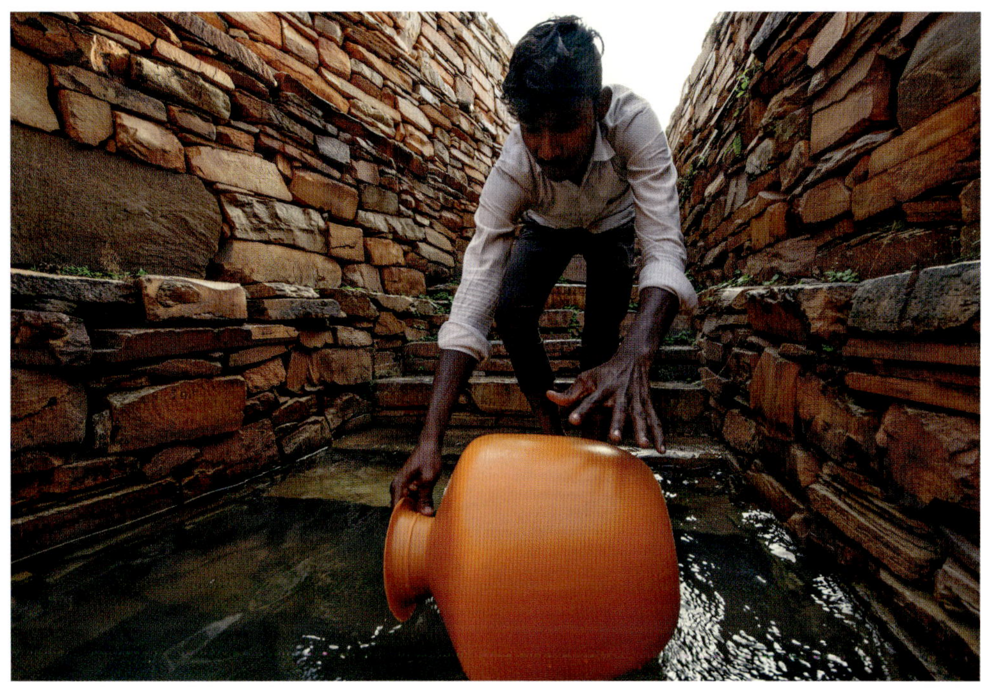

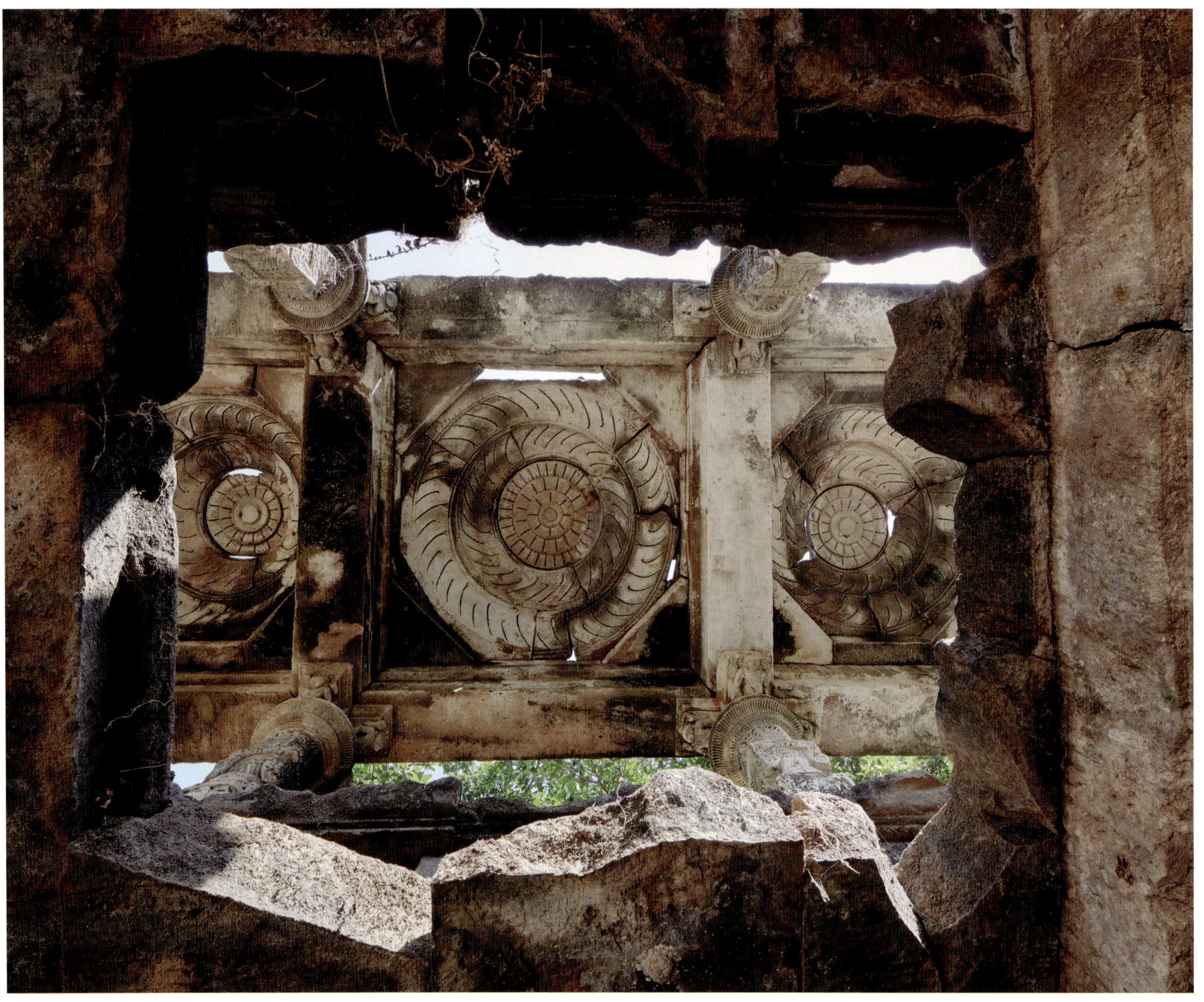

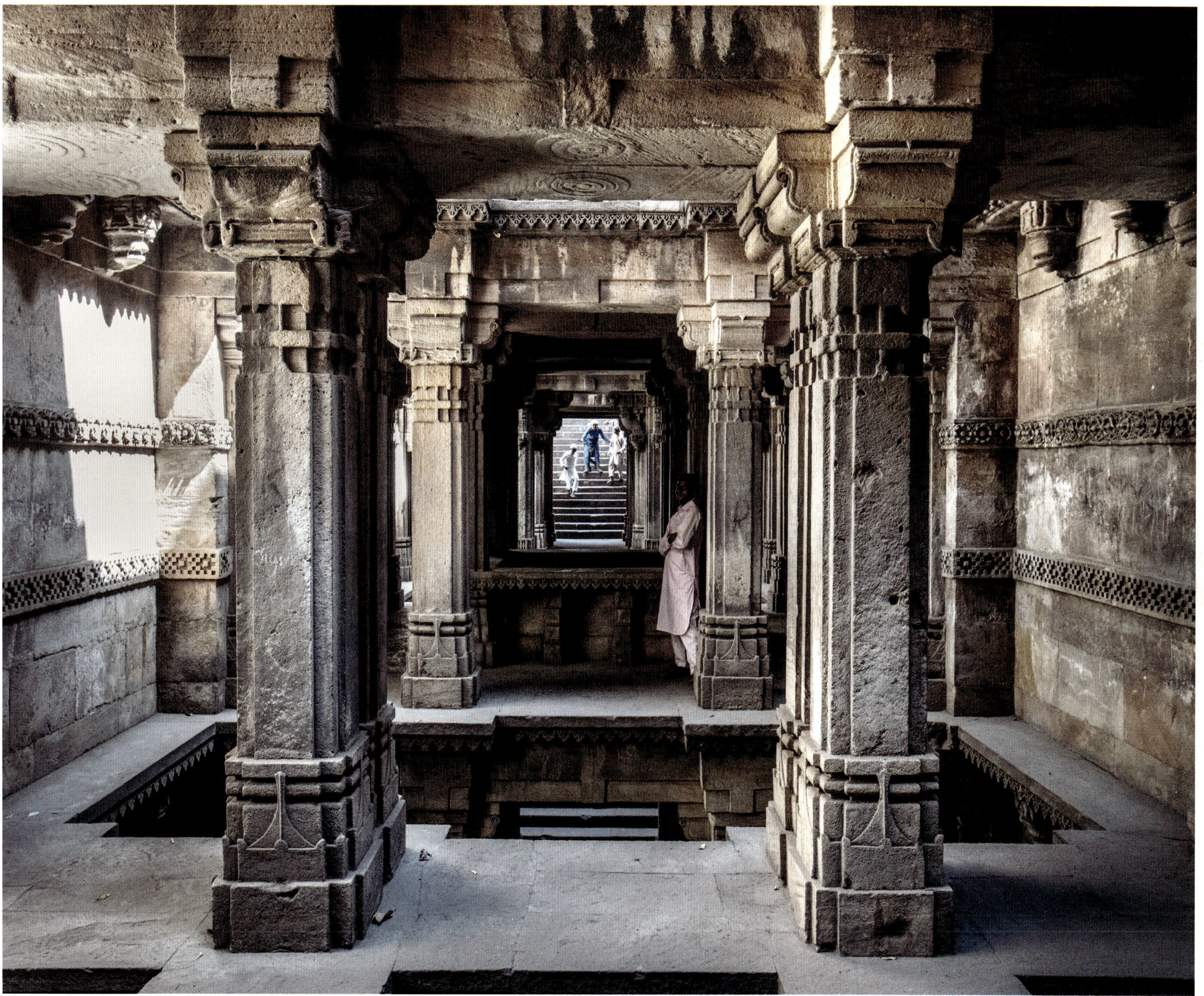

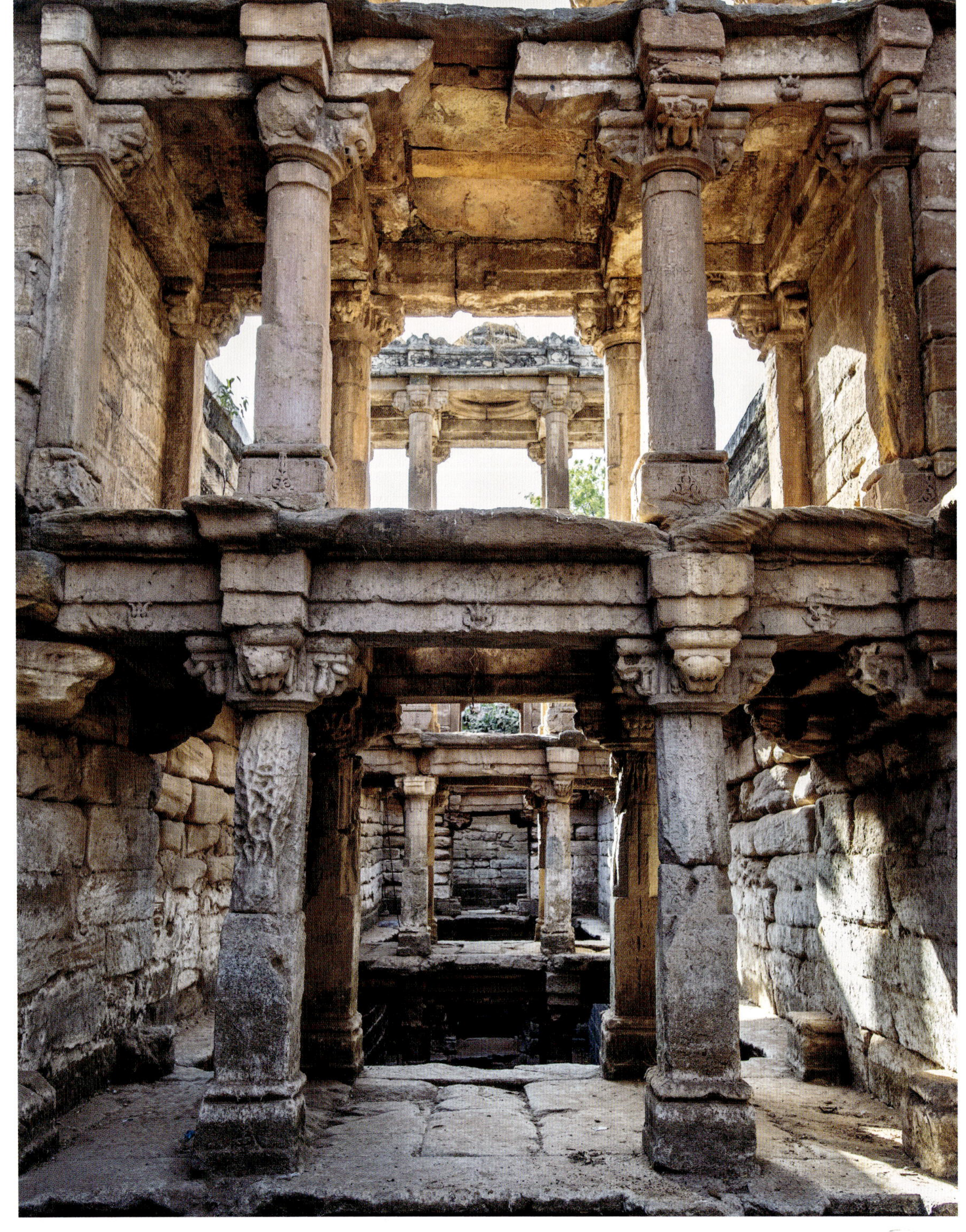

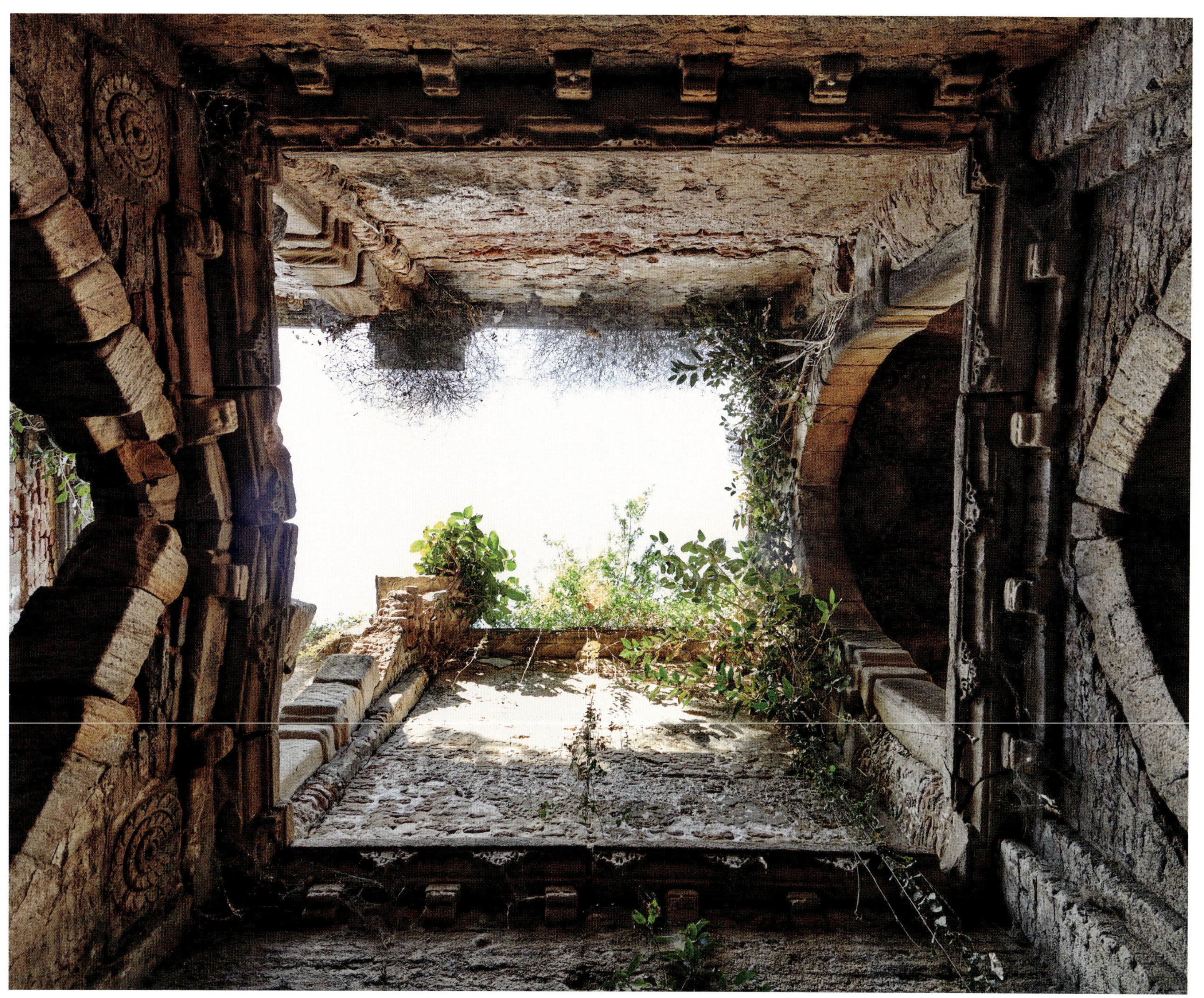

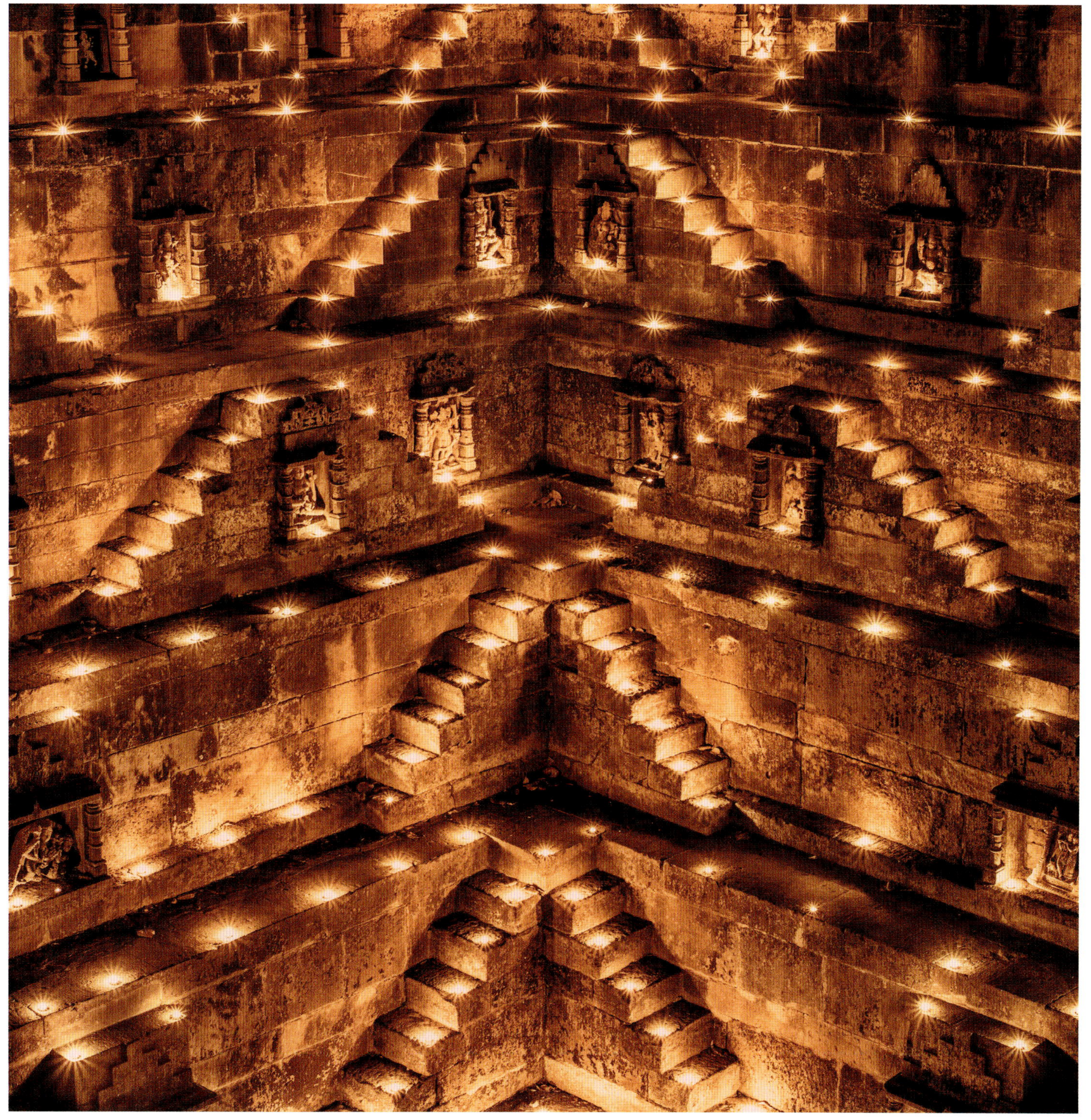

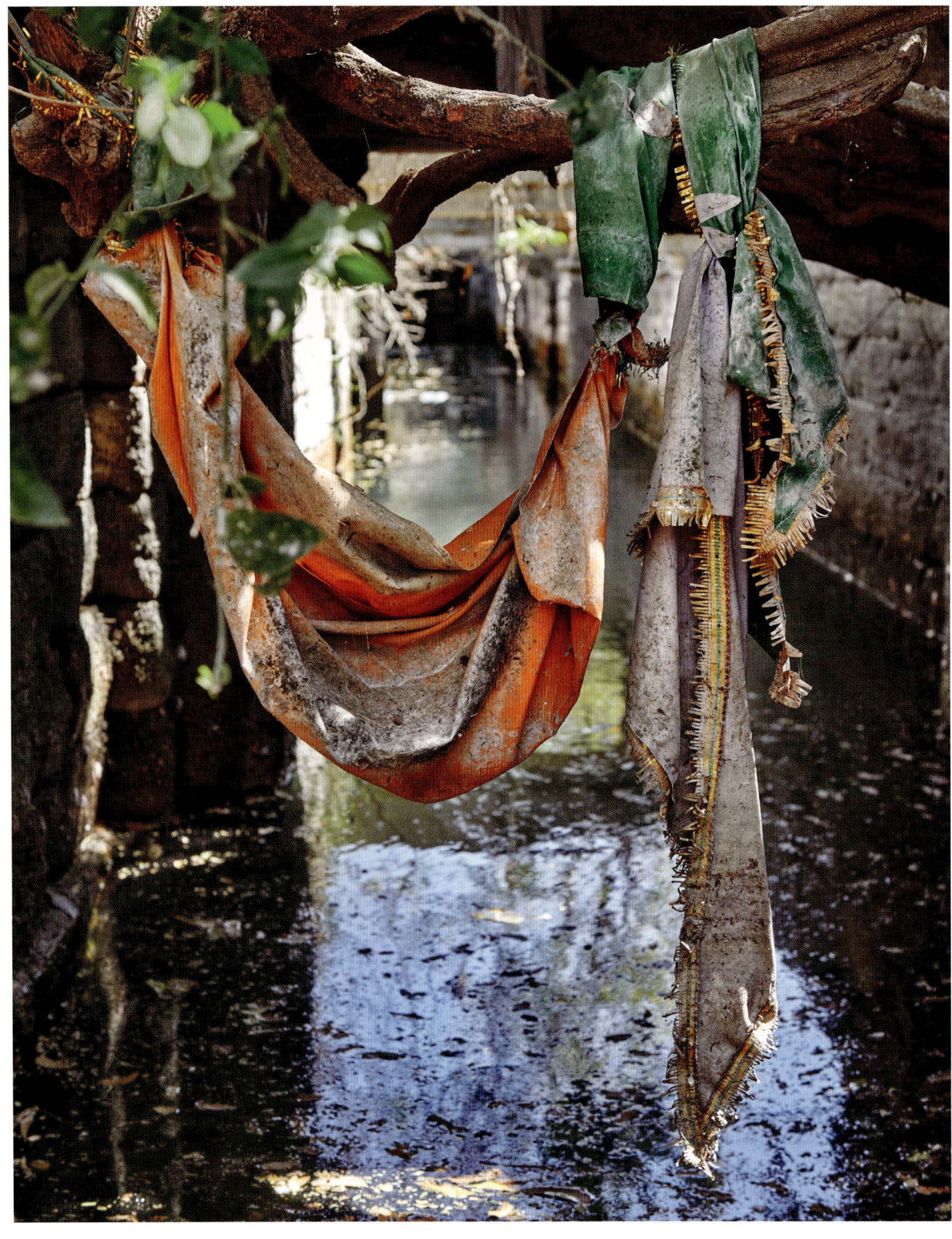

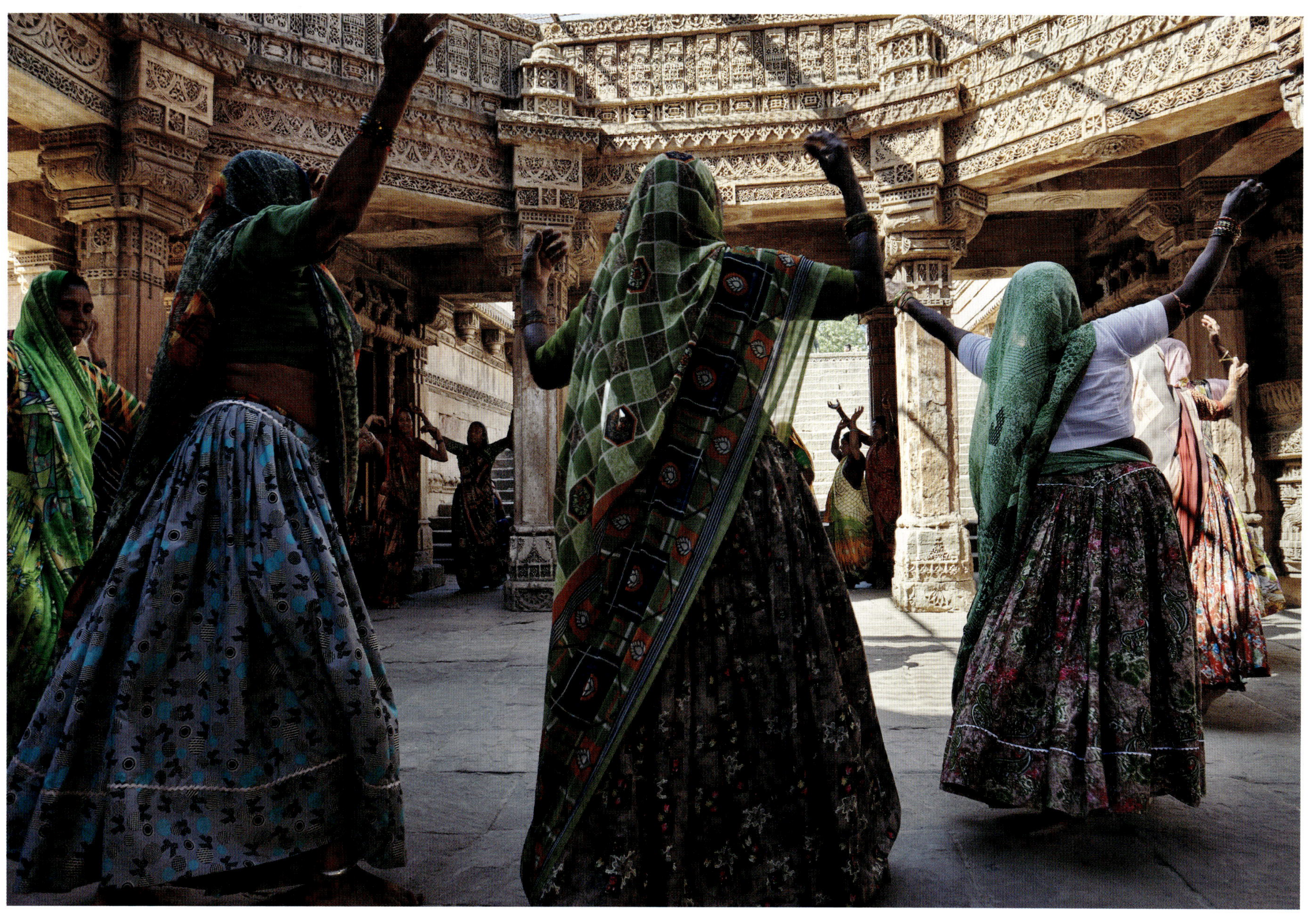

To Reach the Source

I first saw pictures of stepwells in India at an exhibit in Paris in the fall of 2012: delicate Fresson prints of some of the larger and better-known wells across Gujarat and Rajasthan. Intrigued by what I saw, I made a note to myself to try to see one on my next trip to India, but it would take another four years to do so. During a whirlwind trip through Rajasthan that I had organized for my mother, we went from Amber Fort, just north of Jaipur, down into the village of Amer, where the tour book said that there was a stepwell called Panna Meena Kund. When we arrived, we could scarcely believe our eyes. Astonished by the beautiful, Escher-like pattern of its zig-zagging steps leading down to the central basin, I ventured into the well to make some pictures. I emailed one to a friend that same evening, as if to ask for confirmation of the extraordinariness of what I had seen. Sensing my incredulousness, he wrote back right away from halfway around the world to say, "It would be foolish for you not to pursue this further." It would, nevertheless, take me several more years before I finally managed to start this project. And so, in 2019, I began traveling across various parts of India to photograph stepwells of all kinds, in an attempt to understand what they were – and why they were.

Stepwells are fundamentally different from wells as we generally think of them. In most places in the world, a well is a relatively narrow shaft in the ground into which we lower a bucket or install a pump to draw water up to the surface.

The simplicity of its structure mirrors that of its purpose: to facilitate our access to the water that we use to drink, wash, and irrigate. In modern times this has become so efficient and effortless, that we hardly assign any thought to this process or to its practical or symbolic value. This has turned water into little more than a commodity for most of us, something that resides entirely in the realm of the functional, and one that we ignore at that.

Across much of the Indian subcontinent, people have traditionally had a multifaceted relationship to water, in part because a well here is often more than just an inconspicuous work of engineering. With steps that lead directly to the water's edge, it is instead an architecture, an inhabitable space. Some are small and simple in design, with just one flight of stairs going down to a well shaft, while others descend as many as eight or nine stories, the well becoming something like an inverse building. Such structures do exist elsewhere in the world, but only rarely; they are an exception or a folly rather than a consistent practice. In India and some of its neighboring countries, there are thousands of them, and no two are perfectly alike.

People have built stepwells in India for almost two millennia; the earliest surviving examples in western Gujarat contain elements that date back to as early as the fourth century CE. Some are linear, with steps descending to a landing, and then further steps that descend to the next landing, each one of which, thus, has a landing at every level above it. From each flight of steps, in between the skeletal structure of these platforms, one can look up and see the sky. The cylindrical well shaft, or *kuo*, lies at the end of this structure and is open to it on all "stories," from the ground level down to the bottom. These are known in Gujarat as a *vav*. They feel like an open-air church that sinks into the ground. Others have steps that descend back and forth along the four sides of the structure, down and in towards the basin at the bottom, the well shaft submerged at its center. Shaped like inverted pyramids and fully open to the sky, these are known as *kunds,* which comprise all manners of ponds, manmade and not. Others yet take the simple shape of a cylinder with a helical staircase that snakes down along its inner circumference. In Gujarati, these are called *bhammariya*, which refers – even

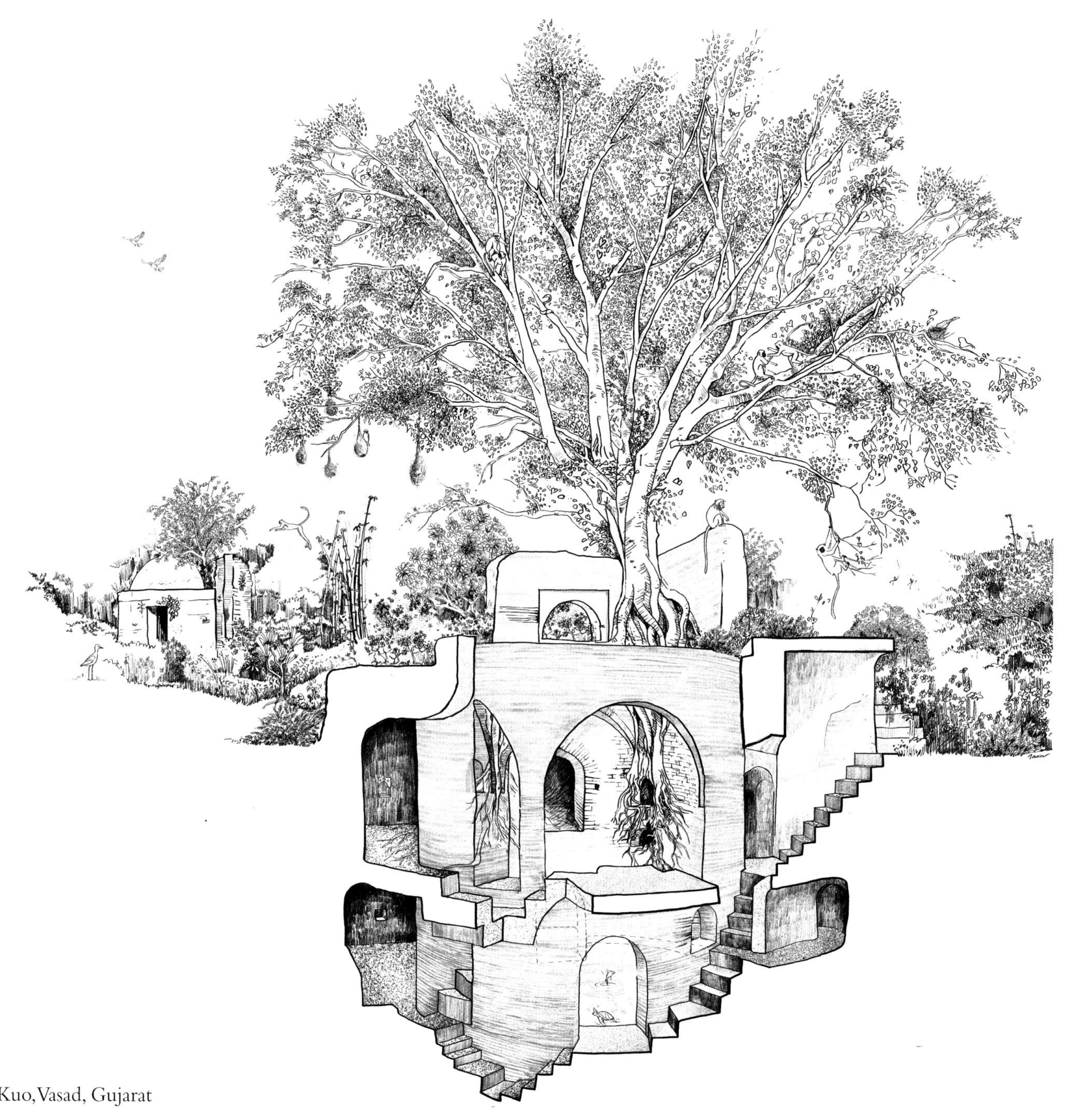

Section, Fer Kuo, Vasad, Gujarat

onomatopoeically – to the upward spiral pattern of a bumblebee's flight. Some are hybrids that combine different aspects of these three types.

They form part of a larger typology of water structures found across India that includes ponds and tanks. At great risk of oversimplifying, stepwells can be distinguished from these other systems for being generally deeper than they are wide. Their size, style, and degree of ornament vary considerably according to the era of their construction and their geography, thus creating a considerable range of forms. But even wells built near each other during the same period as part of a common development project can exhibit differences, however minute. As such, each well feels unique.

Stepwells are a constant source of surprise – and not just because they are a novelty to most people outside the Subcontinent. Most constructions sit above ground, and their volumes are generally perceptible from some distance, be it a house, a Gothic cathedral, or a city skyline. But there is usually little to indicate what shape a stepwell might take, or that it is there at all, even from just a few meters away, as few of them have significant above-ground markers. Only upon arriving at the well's edge can one peer into its depths and discover the mesmerizing geometry of its beautiful form.

And as a stepwell welcomes us below ground, we cannot help but marvel at its architecture, be it humble or monumental, or plain or elaborate. Its ambiance affects all of our senses. Walking down the steps, the space becomes quieter, removed from the distracting boisterousness of daily life. Our footsteps, breaths, and words resonate so much more, to the point of echoing. A properly tended well smells invitingly fresh, perhaps earthy, but not dirty. The temperature descends pleasantly, becoming cool but never cold, a welcome change from the often oppressive heat. Free of the dust and pollution that seems to circulate everywhere above ground, the humid air feels cleaner too. Sunlight shifts less perceptibly within the well, and with that, one's sense of time blurs somewhat, the minutes and the hours flowing by effortlessly as one contemplates the impressive surrounding structure, and the water within it. This sensation of immersing oneself within a space – which in turn is immersed in the water – becomes a kind of open-eyed meditation. It is like seeing a reflection of our world on the surface, but from within that reflection.

And because they are largely open structures, the sky is never far away. Looking up from the very bottom of a well feels a little like gazing out of the cratered pools in Mexico's Yucatan Peninsula known as *cenotes*. Descending from the surface into this other world, we feel removed from our usual plane of existence, but we are not cut off from it, the way we would be upon entering a parking garage, for example; such spaces, however ordinary, suggest that we are going down into some sort of netherworld. And at a well's deepest and dimmest point, we once again find the sky reflected in the water. This experience of inversion is magical and expansive instead of uncomfortable or even fearful. We are not going away from life, instead towards it.

Because the water table in much of India varies considerably over the course of the year, a stepwell is an amphibious space, and this is part of its fascination. With the monsoon rains and ensuing saturation of the ground, the many levels of a well become submerged, resurfacing again as the water level slowly recedes after the rains stop, no worse for the wear, requiring just a cursory cleaning each year and a more thorough de-silting every now and then. The steps always lead to the water's edge, regardless of its level. The only spaces I have seen outside India that produce this same Atlantis-like effect are the Greco-Roman cisterns in cities such as Istanbul and Naples, even though they are ultimately sealed off from the sun and the world above ground.

The water itself is cool and refreshing. Although it may appear stagnant, it is in fact moving, because it seeps through the ground and stone to enter the well. And the more water that people take, the more it circulates. There may be a scattering of leaves or branches floating on the top, but this does not mean that the water is dirty; it is in fact often perfectly clear below the surface. People who still draw water from stepwells simply sweep the surface with their forearms to clear any floating debris before submerging their water jugs to fill them.

In some cases, people add fish to a well to help keep the water free of algae and other growths. The presence of other creatures such as frogs and turtles is considered auspicious, as is shown by the relief sculptures of such aquatic animals embedded in the curved wall of the well shaft. This presumably celebrates the well as a vital space. For the people who built and used these wells, the water is a living, dynamic part of the natural world, and the more life it contains, the healthier and purer it is perceived to be. In modern, industrial society, we have come to view water as a distilled essence that should be free of all other things, and its abstract delivery through our plumbing pipes only heightens this sense of its denaturing to the point of lifelessness. Water in a stepwell is not just a symbol of life; it is itself alive.

Each time I have entered a stepwell, my amazement has always given way to the same question, namely, why build such complex structures? Why not, for the sake of simplicity, just dig a hole into the ground, as almost all other peoples have?

The necessity of such structures is readily apparent. Much of the Subcontinent is hot and semi-arid, and rains tend to fall in high concentrations within the brief period of the monsoon each summer. There is a general paucity of naturally accumulating surface water in many regions. As such, a dependable source of groundwater was paramount to a community's viability. In fact, people often sank a well before deciding whether to establish any sort of settlement, thus making the well its first permanent structure. But why did people expend so much additional effort and expense to make these large and often elaborate spaces? Dug wells do abound in India, so it is not that people were in any way hindered from building such simpler structures.

Other practical explanations come to mind. The larger volume of a stepwell allows for a more capacious rainwater harvesting. The well thus becomes a cistern that captures and stores a greater amount of water than what a simple shaft well can accumulate. For being stored below ground, the water also evaporates less than at the surface, as it instead risks doing in a reservoir.

Stone backrests and viewing pavilions reveal their social nature, that they were a place for people to gather and meet, especially during the hot months, when the coolness of the stepwell offered much needed respite. Their public nature meant that they were open to residents and travelers alike. Built along trade routes that ran from the Arabian Sea across Gujarat and the entire Deccan plateau, they provided itinerant merchants with a place to break journey and water their beasts of burden, a kind of caravanserai. As monuments, we can imagine rulers eager to assert their presence and foster allegiances, or the lavishness of patrons who sought to benefit their community – and lavish they often were, as such wells were sometimes the biggest, most ornate building in a settlement.

And yet, important as such large public works were for a society, for all the above reasons, there were perhaps just as many practical reasons not to build such intricate structures. Why, for example, did builders in many cases haul massive stones, sometimes from dozens of kilometers away and by oxcart at that, not even by boat, given the absence of a nearby waterway? And why decorate the wells with so much carved ornament, all of which rendered the building process so much more complex and expensive?

To understand stepwells better, it helps if we step outside our contemporary mindset, starting with our sense of time. Our current notions of what is "practical" or "efficient" tend to assess cost and effort mainly in terms of an immediate yield. Stepwells were instead a long-term infrastructural investment in a community's sustenance and sustainability. They were built to last, and there was nothing obsolescent about them. In fact, many centuries later, these wells are often still in excellent condition – and when they are not, one can frequently point to recent, human-induced phenomena as the cause of their weakening or decay.

But even allowing for such farsightedness, a stepwell can still often seem bigger, more monumental, and more ornate than it needs to be, to our pragmatist eyes. We do better if we instead reflect simply on what the beauty of these underground spaces evokes in us, compared to our other descents below the surface, which generally feel claustrophobic, if not somewhat tomb-like.

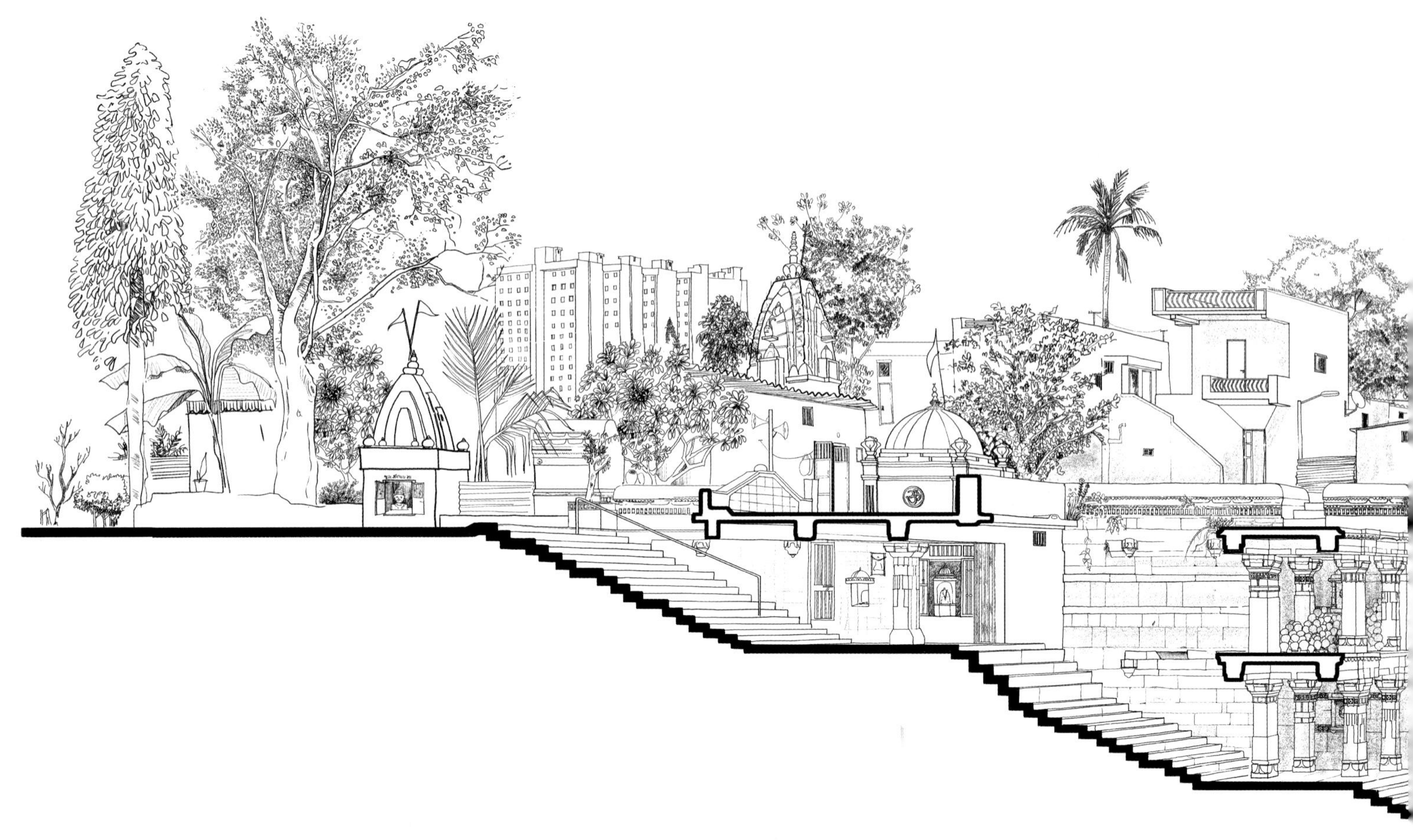

Section, Ashapura Mata Ni Vav, Bapunagar, Ahmedabad, Gujarat

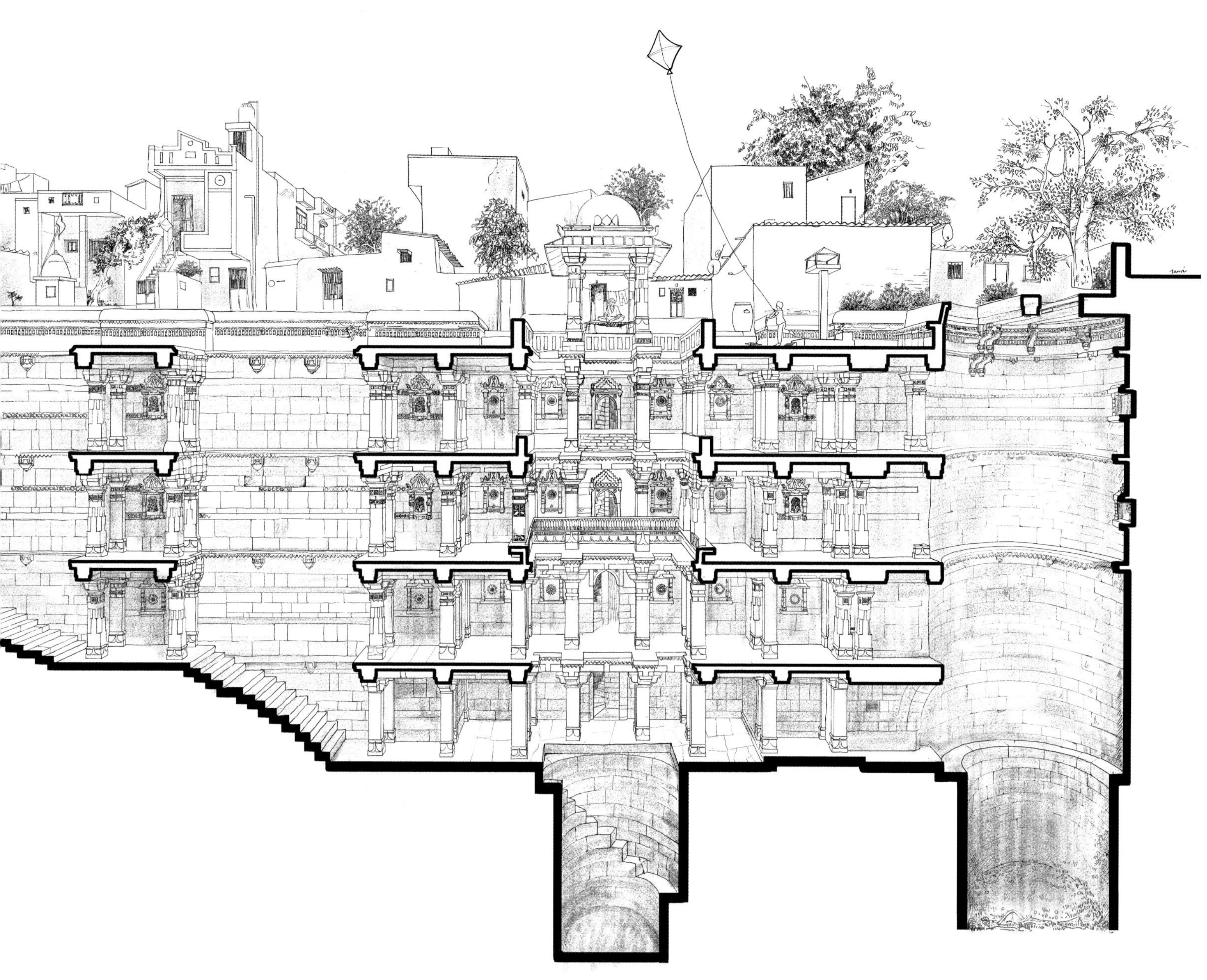

We are not merely in the realm of necessity. Here instead, we feel pleasure and comfort, if not wonder, at where we are in the world.

Which ultimately is in a kind of temple, especially when we consider the many altar-like structures and statues of divinities the wells contain. Many, if not most cultures sacralize the presence of water below ground, viewing it as something miraculous. But in most places around the world, such subterranean spaces tend to be left in their rough, dark, and natural state, which is not necessarily inviting. What is instead so unique about a stepwell is that people built a rational, aesthetic framework to enshrine and ritualize this approach to water. It is more than a place that facilitates how we fetch water; it changes our very relationship to it in experiential terms. The architecture provides more than accessibility; it creates a relationship to water that is dynamic and direct.

We can thus touch the water at the source, drink it, even immerse ourselves in it. We can enjoy simply being close to it, contemplating it within this magnificent and comfortable space, the same way people might pray next to the tomb of a Sufi saint in a shrine or before a statue in a church, reveling in their proximity to a divine phenomenon or essence. A stepwell renders the water's many meanings manifest, immanent, palpable; the space encourages us to become mindful of the essential, sacred nature of water, even though this life force or energy is not personified or named. It provides a kind of *darshan*, the moment when a Hindu devotee experiences a connection with the divine and comes to feel blessed. Some stepwells were referred to as a *tirtha*, a Sanskrit word that literally means a river crossing, a place of passage from one place to another, and which is commonly used to describe the destination of a pilgrimage, a place that grants purification and enlightenment.

A stepwell is thus a functional space *and* a religious one, all at once. Many cultures, including most Western ones, tend to separate these roles in their built environments, but a stepwell combines the practical with the spiritual, as wonderfully often happens in India.

Aesthetically pleasing as a stepwell is, the water does retain a sense of power and formidability. The stonework may encase the water and, thus, help us use it and contemplate what it means to us, but it does not repress the element's force in any way. Especially when the well is full, the water can feel immeasurably deep and, as such, menacing. The water retains a sense of the sublime, but the architecture ultimately mutes our dread into awe, and this expands our experience of it. The magnificently cool water of a stepwell is regenerative, both in a profane and a sacred sense. It nourishes and refreshes us, and it also purifies and renews us. We are ritually reborn in the water of a well. Immersing ourselves, even if only by looking at it, symbolically reenacts our own genesis in the water of our mothers' wombs.

The stepwell shapes our experience of the water, such that we are not overwhelmed by its formlessness and the threat of dissolving within it. The water tells us that we live and die, but the beauty and the rationality of the architecture remind us that we do more than function biologically; it tells us that we exist, that we have a soul, and that we form part of a larger sense of harmony and order. This sense of rebirth provides transcendence. For Christians, this is akin to the experience of baptism, and for Buddhists, such an experience of water is an acknowledgment of our surrendering one's ego to a larger, serene sense of being.

Perhaps it is not just life but the existence of all matter that is celebrated in such a space. When I visited the eight-spiral well in Walur, Maharashtra, a local pandit told me that the well symbolizes the creation of the cosmos, because in Hinduism, our being is formed of eight elements, the *Ashta Prakriti*. And because this well looks like a Fibonacci spiral galaxy, it was hard to disagree.

The aesthetic, metaphysical, and cosmogonic experience of a stepwell has very strong female connotations. Cultures generally view the creative, life-giving force within the ground, and specifically within water, as eminently feminine, and India is no exception. It is in fact Mother Earth to most peoples. Agriculture is a goddess in most ancient cultures, in Greece and elsewhere. Life springs forth from her. But as much as cultures revere this power and energy, they also tend to view it as amorphous and incomprehensible. This has also translated into a fear of the feminine. We could say that the inaccessibility of a narrow, deep, dark well that we look down into with both fascination and foreboding only aggravates this. The beautiful, often grandiose, and ultimately accessible structure of a stepwell is instead a way to engage with this life force, to come close to it, to understand and ultimately to embrace it, to respect and venerate it rather than to fear it, and to restore its rightful place in the mythic, cosmic balance of ground and sky, which we generally think of as respectively female and male.

Indeed, stepwells are in many ways spaces about, for, and by women. Many wells in Gujarat, for example, are named for female Hindu deities; it is rarer to find wells named for the Brahminic male gods. In Akhaj, Gujarat, there is a magnificent stepwell known as Shakti Kund, *Shakti* referring to the female divine essence that manifests itself through all the goddesses in the Hindu pantheon. The many statues in this well are mainly of female deities and women in various positions, even in childbirth. And when we see the unique shape of the well in Mailacherla, in remote Andhra Pradesh, which at once suggests the devotional candle known as a *diya*, a drop of water, and the labia of a vagina, we see to the extent to which stepwells embody and sacralize the power of the feminine.

This has manifested itself in the history of the wells' construction too. Women, either rulers or wealthy members of their communities, often commissioned the wells, as evidenced by the surviving commemorative plaques embedded in the walls at their entrances. As women were responsible for most domestic tasks, we can readily surmise that they brought water to the house and were as such the wells' main users. Stepwells allowed women to congregate in a public space they perhaps did not otherwise navigate or occupy on their own, much like the village oven for women in rural southern Italy, for example. These powerful patrons thus also sought to honor and celebrate this fact by giving women a space of their own. This includes some of India's most important wells, such as Rani Ki Vav in Patan (the most grandiose of them all, in fact) and Dada Harir in Ahmedabad. And although we have almost no specific records of who their builders were, I like to think that women were among their architects as well.

Any sense of unease and remove that we might experience upon entering a stepwell in the present day comes, if anything, from its relative abandonment. The benches with backrests around the various levels of a central well shaft offer a lonesome echo of so much human activity that no longer happens with any regularity. Even restored wells that have been turned into monuments and which receive a good number of tourists throughout the day elicit the distinct sensation that the well was once occupied in a different way, and more fully. Tourists visiting a stepwell may marvel at its architecture, but they usually don't linger in it long enough to inhabit it as people once did. Said another way, people come to see the geometry, but they don't always stay long enough to experience the space.

When British colonialists started surveying stepwells in India in the nineteenth century, they detected guinea worm in some of the structures. They also later accused them of being breeding grounds for the malaria-carrying anopheles mosquito. This impelled a hygienist campaign that resulted in the installation of a village tap for many settlements, one that was connected by pipe plumbing to a presumably parasite-free water source. However, people continued to use and frequent stepwells even after the introduction of this modern "convenience," as stepwells served so many purposes in people's daily lives in addition to supplying water. The flustered British supposedly then threw trash into the wells, and this appears to have broken the spell. This probably defiled them, made them untouchable. Sadly, in our contemporary era of mass waste, this habit has persisted, as many of them remain dumping grounds that one can scarcely enter. Many other wells were filled in.

In fact, human actions often seem to be the main reason for the stepwells' demise, more than just the wear and tear of time, as they are generally very soundly built. For example, the stepwells in Gujarat were constructed with interlocking stones to resist the severe earthquakes that befall this region. While the 2001 earthquake razed many above-ground structures in the historic city of Bhuj and its environs, most stepwells in the region remained unaffected, as their flexible structure moved with the shaking earth and absorbed its shocks.

Building encroachment is a much more direct cause of structural weakening. Whereas stepwells preserved some measure of space around them even after they fell into disuse, the often uncontrolled urban development of the last few decades has resulted in the construction of buildings right next to a stepwell. The weight of these newer, larger structures exerts a downward pressure which then pushes inward against the sides of the well, eventually causing walls to bulge and beams to collapse; the carefully calculated balance of forces that the stepwell had maintained for centuries is thus upset, if not terminally compromised.

Falling water tables are also to blame for their destabilization. In many cases the drilling of many deeper bore wells to supply a growing population with ready access to plumbed water has depressed the aquifer to far below the wells' levels throughout the year, leaving them only momentarily wetted by a rainwater that they fail to withhold from the thirsty ground beneath them. This too throws off the balance of forces.

Thus, along with the pleasant surprise of discovering a stepwell can also come dismay, if not disgust at its condition. When the water table leaves the well dry year-round, it feels empty and obsolete, devoid of its essential function, almost lifeless. And when there is water in the well shaft, it is sometimes choked with plastic bottles and bags, snack wrappers, and other detritus. Without a constant human presence, animals such as pigeons or bats can colonize them, adding a significant level of filth and stench. Territorial cobras sometimes appropriate wells, which, of course, further discourages visits. Along with the inevitable erosion that time brings, especially to the ornamentation, this abandonment yields a sense of rot, of a muddy mortality.

All this decay compromises their beauty, but it does not fully undo it. While indulging in a sense of elegy in my pictures, I also try to accept what is broken about the wells, because they still feel alive, albeit with their diseased gums and missing teeth. Sometimes friends and I clean up a well before taking pictures, hoping the garbage we amass at the top of the well will somehow be taken elsewhere and not just kicked back down the steps after we leave. There are no organized means of inorganic trash disposal in many of these out-of-the-way places, which is part of the reason why wells, viewed as holes in the ground, tend to attract waste.

We are often the only visitors to a well, but not always. Most often, teenage boys use them as backdrops to make TikTok videos of themselves. In wells that sit next to a temple, devotees may appropriate the altars inside the well to venerate a deity; this annexation brings people down into the space, even if just a little. Here and there, one sees a young couple going all the way down to the water's edge. It is safe to assume that they are seeking a fertility blessing, as people probably always have. The rituals feel more scattered than they once were when such practices were more constant, but a sense of the sacred endures, in however frail and fragmentary a manner.

Above ground, people are generally aware that they possess a significant piece of heritage, but it remains removed from most aspects of their daily lives. Local residents are certainly happy for our visits, all the more so at our appreciation of the beauty of their well, regardless of its state, but in most cases, they do not come down into the well with us to explore it, waiting above ground for us to reemerge from its deeper levels. Children are especially hesitant. When pressed, many of them say that their mothers have told them that a large snake inhabits the well, and that they are therefore too scared to enter, a clever parental tactic (although it does also echo Indian cosmogonic myths in which primeval snakes help to churn the world into existence). Ultimately, some essential thing remains broken in many such cases.

And as people have lost reasons to go into a well, they usually lack the resources at the local level to restore or even repurpose the well in a way

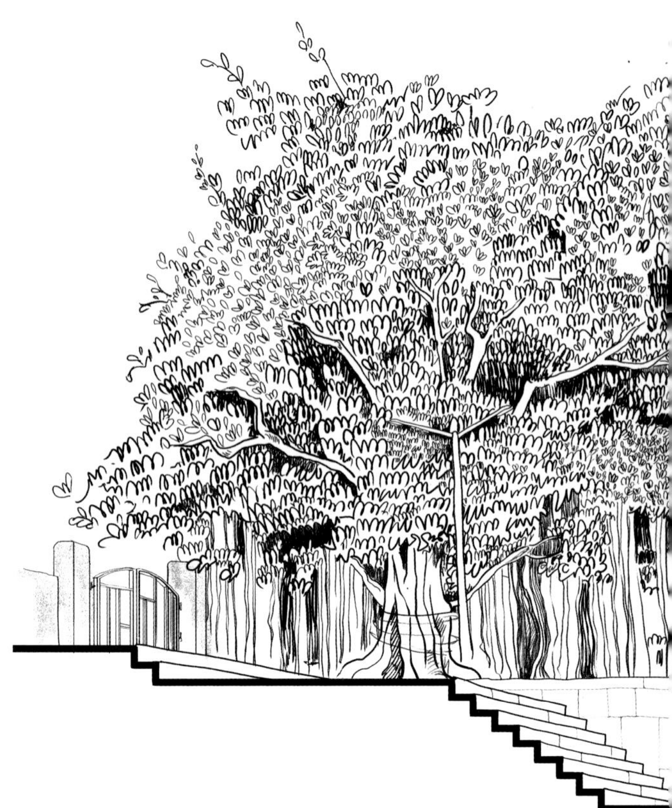

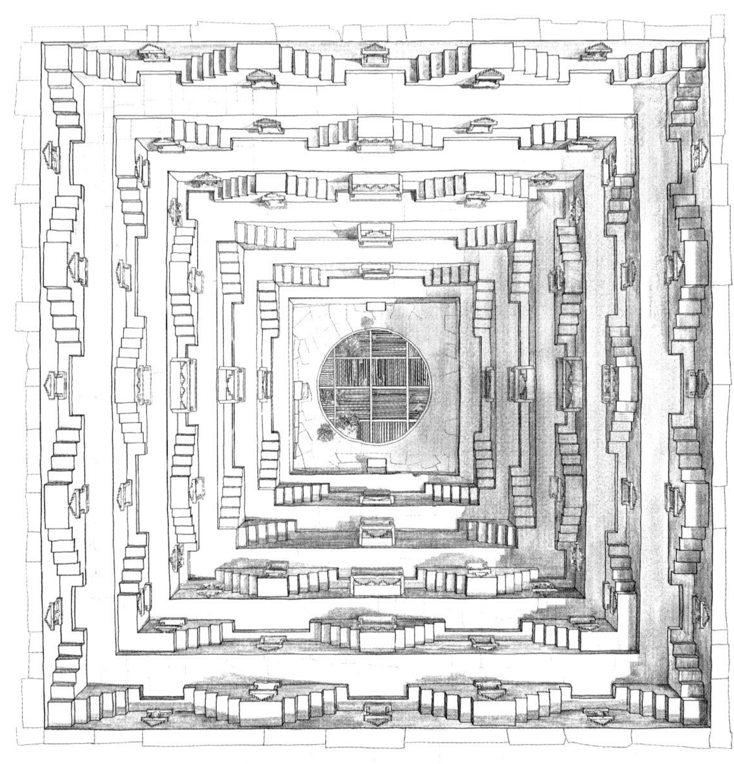

Plan and Section, Shakti Kund, Akhaj, Gujarat

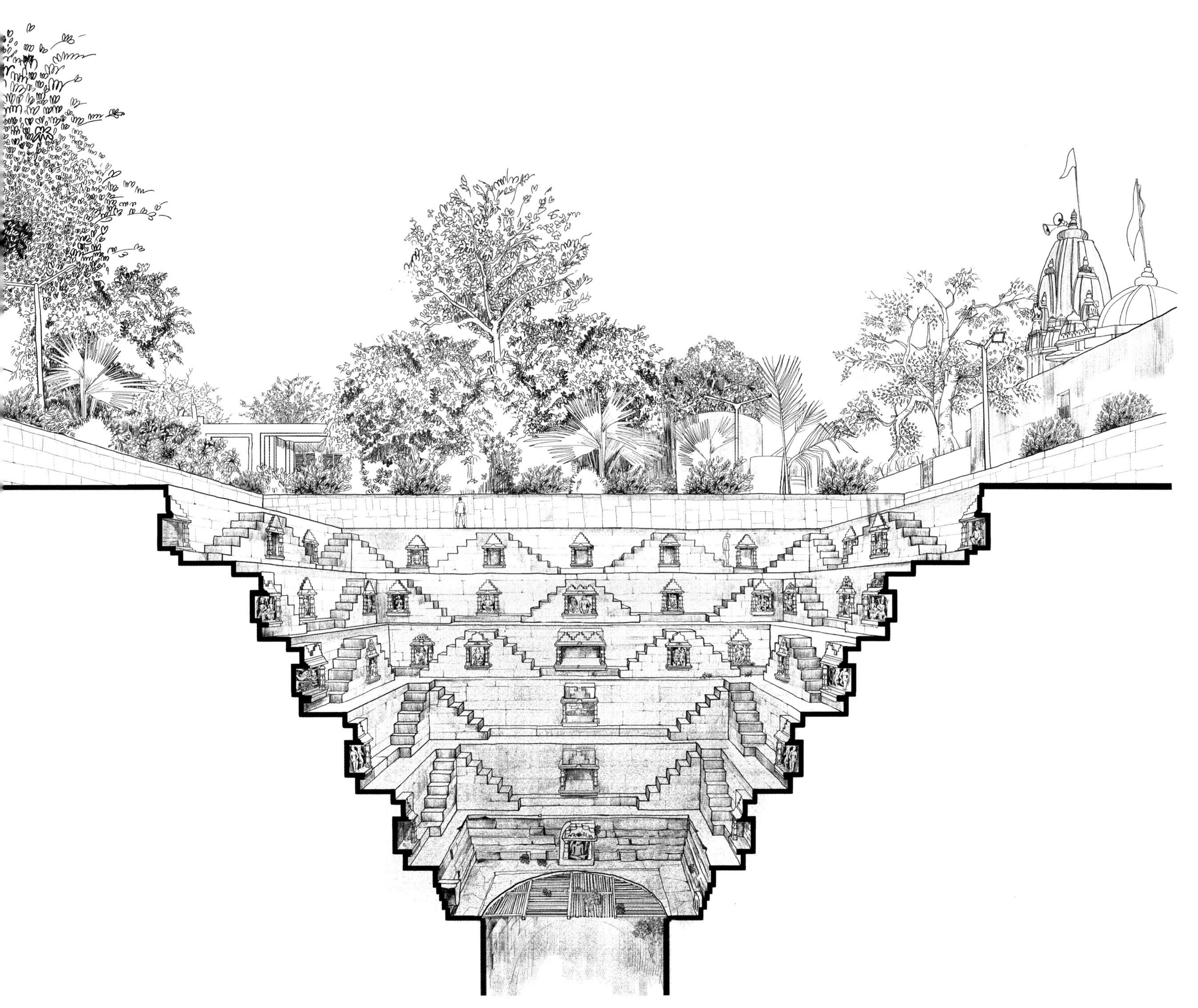

that would entice people back into the space. Historically and aesthetically important as they are, it is not immediately possible in most cases for the government and society to restore them as part of an economically virtuous circle of preservation and tourism that would justify that expense in the long term, especially for the many that are located in out-of-the-way places. There are far more wells in need of repair than the Indian Archaeological Survey can get to in the short-term.

Happily, more and more initiatives are being undertaken at all levels to restore stepwells. As one example among many, Toorji Ka Jhalra Baori, a stepwell in Jodhpur's city center, now functions as a kind of swimming pool and meeting place where young people come to sit on the steps of this large, beautiful, and cool space, socializing and watching divers leap from more than ten meters above into the water. Architecture and heritage advocacy groups in various Indian cities have been successfully lobbying for the restoration of stepwells. In Hyderabad, this led to the transformation of the once decrepit Bansalipet stepwell into a magnificent public space, and then to the restoration of a further 30 wells throughout the city by a number of local and international groups, including the Aga Khan Foundation. Grassroots efforts led by architects, photographers, and heritage activists to revive stepwells outside major city centers appear to be proliferating across the country.

One does encounter a minority of wells that are properly tended to and even used to varying productive extents. Some have pipes going down to the bottom of the well shaft that mechanically pump out water, either for homes or to irrigate fields. In such a case, people have simply spared themselves the walk up and down, but they are still using the well. And a select few wells, like the *diya*-shaped *kund* in Mailacherla, Andhra Pradesh, have remained intact in form and function. Three hundred years after this unique structure was first built in this tiny village located at the end of a dirt track, at the edge of a large forest, it remains structurally sound, in almost perfect condition. The 70 or so inhabitants of this remote community continue to fetch their drinking water here one or more times a day, and to swim in it when it is full.

The construction of large stepwells had largely halted by the time the British arrived in India in the eighteenth century. But they do continue to be dug on a small scale in various parts of the country, especially in Karnataka, where the Bhovi community of well diggers still builds simple but beautiful helical wells, mainly in the countryside. Their skills and experience, reduced to a core but still intact, are now also in demand in the city. Bangalore's current urban development regulations mandate that all new constructions be accompanied by several shallow wells, three to six meters deep, to capture rainwater channeled from building roofs and elsewhere. Use of these "recharge wells" lessens the reliance on the deep bore wells that are depressing the water table, and which ultimately risk exhausting it in the dry season, as is increasingly happening in major cities such as Bangalore and Chennai.

Climate change poses many risks to India's sustainability already today. At certain times of the year, temperatures are approaching the limits of human survivability in many places. Taking refuge underground may prove helpful or necessary for millions of people in such circumstances, providing them with access to water and cooler temperatures. Stepwells offer a functional and aesthetic model for a kind of shelter that can help increase our climate resilience.

The fate of many of these structures remains uncertain because there may not be enough resources or social and political will to rehabilitate them. But there are many reasons to do so, from the functional to the social, the environmental, the historical, and the aesthetic. The mindfulness of water they generate in us is essential to our living well, both in terms of our survival and our sense of our place in the world. Once an integral part of people's culture, they may once again prove so in the future. Like the rains that return each year, the lives of the stepwells themselves may also prove cyclical.

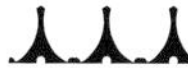

The few stepwell-like constructions that exist outside India do emulate some of the same forms and principles as their Indian counterparts. The closest one in spirit to an Indian stepwell that I have ever seen is in the Water Synagogue in Úbeda, Spain, in the very north of Andalusia: a rare, early mikveh, a Jewish ritual purification bath, which dates to at least the Middle Ages. Mikvehs must fill naturally, which tends to mean that they are located below ground, and in turn that they likely form part of a built space providing access to the bath. In this case, the mikveh is two levels below ground, the first underground floor occupied by the former synagogue. Most extraordinarily, on the day of the summer solstice, the sun shines in through a doorway and a now glassed-in opening in the floor to illuminate the seven steps hewn out of the stone that lead down to the half-meter of water that fills the mikveh's basin year-round.

The island of Sardinia has a series of stepwell structures that date back some three millennia, all of which follow the same typology. The best preserved and the most beautiful is the well of Santa Cristina in Paulilatino, which descends one flight of narrowing stairs into a cylindrical enclosure whose dome sits above ground level. On the spring and fall equinoxes, the sun shines directly down the stairs and through the small oculus on the top of the dome to illuminate the water precisely from both directions. Every 18.5 years, during a "lunistice," the full moon performs the same feat, mirroring itself precisely in the water. This has prompted some scholars to wonder whether these wells also served as observatories.

Very interestingly, the dating of the stone cuts in the walls directly around and above the Úbeda mikveh has led archaeologists to theorize that it too originally sat within a larger domed structure that may be much older than the synagogue itself – and perhaps even an expression of this same archetype – which was partially preserved as it became agglomerated into newer constructions.

Older civilizations outside India thus appeared to share this impulse, using a somewhat similar architectural form, to consecrate a relationship to water that lies below ground, and to view it as connected to the sky, and not removed from it. Through their astronomical precision (which may be greater than what we find in Indian stepwells), these older structures share a similar desire to align themselves with a larger sense of order and beauty in the cosmos. Much as at neolithic sites like Stonehenge, we can feel their builders wanting to understand and celebrate their place in the universe, to commemorate a sense of unity with and among the remotest of its elements. Here too, the well is more than a well, as we now tend to think of it; its beauty is an expression of the sacred.

So, in contemplating the marvel of a stepwell's construction, the question to ask may not be so much, why did people build these? We might instead wonder, why did so many of us outside India stop?

"Please get me some apples," my mother would say. Some of my least favorite words as a child, even if this request might result in a dessert I was sure to love. They were stored in a small closet in the very back of the basement, a cold, eerie space that contained few things – a laundry, winter sleds not in use, some jars of jam, old clothes – but which otherwise felt cut off from everything and everyone else. I of course feared that ghosts lurked down there, waiting to catch me alone and do who knows what to me. No one would hear. The fact that the furnace would occasionally rumble to diabolical life right as I ventured by it only heightened my uneasiness. I would turn on every light as I went through the various doors, all the way to the very back corner, the farthest from our life above ground. My mother would ask me why I always raced back up the stairs at breakneck speed, sometimes dropping one of the apples, which I would then have to go back down to retrieve. As a child in WWII Germany, she had spent many nights in a cellar that served as a bomb shelter for the family, but to my amazement, she could go into the basement even without turning on a single light.

I only recall one instance when I was not scared of this space. After starting swimming lessons, I asked my parents whether we could flood the basement to turn it into a pool. I would handle all the details. In my mind, this would be not only luxuriant, but also comfortable and reassuring. And ghosts couldn't swim in that fullness.

Wells were equally mysterious to me at that age. Our water at home was delicious, better than anywhere else, a gift from some world below that I could not picture clearly. But it was limited, and we were often at risk of running out. When my parents decided to sink a second well, neighbors suggested we call old Mr. Dodge to tell us exactly where to drill. He was a dowser, a "water witch," they said. He had found water for just about everyone in the area who had asked him. On the given day, he arrived with a forked stick of smooth wood. He walked around, holding his wishbone-shaped implement pointed upwards, one hand on each branch, thumbs down, elbows jutting out. In one spot, his wrists appeared to snap quickly and the stick flipped down, pointing towards the ground. "Found it!" he told us with a smile. Sensing our incredulity, he asked if anyone wanted to hold the divining rod with him. When he walked with my brother over the designated spot, the stick again flipped down suddenly. My brother said there was nothing he could do to stop it. It was over before he knew, like losing an arm-wrestle in a split-second. That day, we could all feel the magnetic presence of the water below us. But I still couldn't see it. I knew that it was, but I still wondered what it was.

Some forty years later, my fears were washed away and my curiosity was gratified as I stood at the edge of a stepwell in Rajasthan, gazing at the beautiful answer.

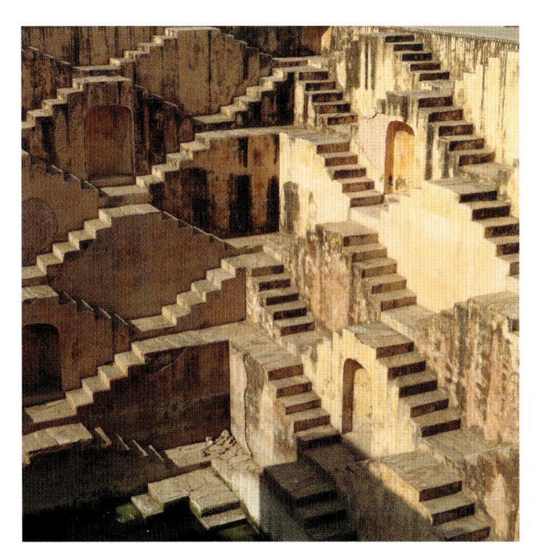

List of images

with an indication of the well's name, location, and date of construction
All wells were photographed between February 2019 and February 2023.

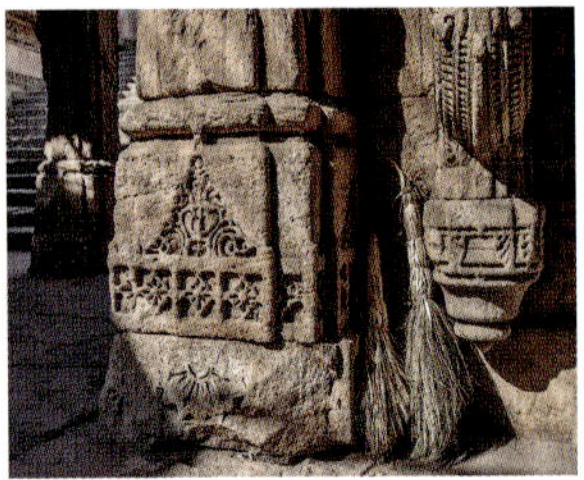

Page 20
Queen Rudabai Vav
Adalaj, Gujarat
1498 CE

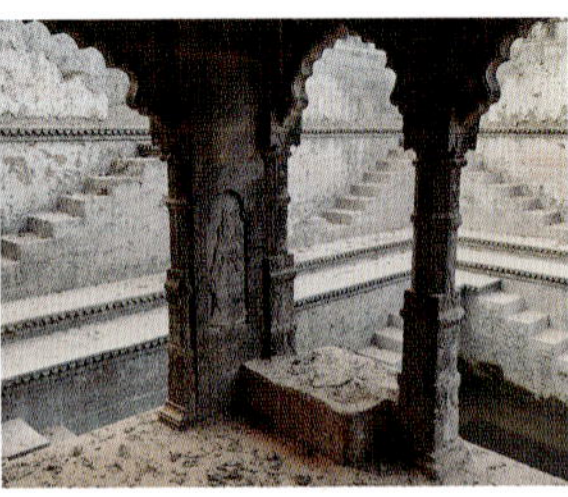

Page 21
Talab Gaon Baoli
Bundi, Rajasthan
18th-19th centuries

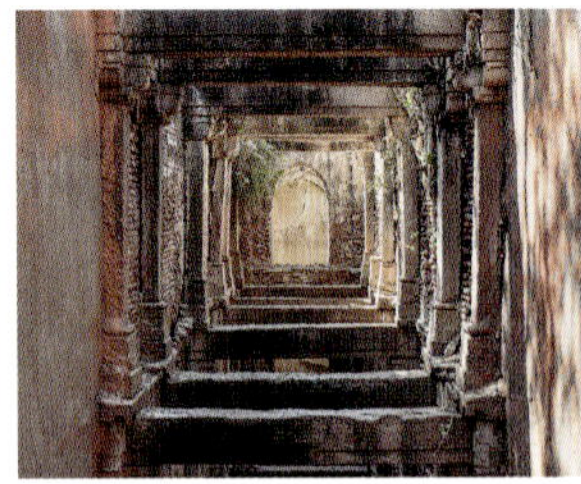

Page 22
Uvarsad Ni Vav
Uvarsad, Gujarat
ca. 17th century

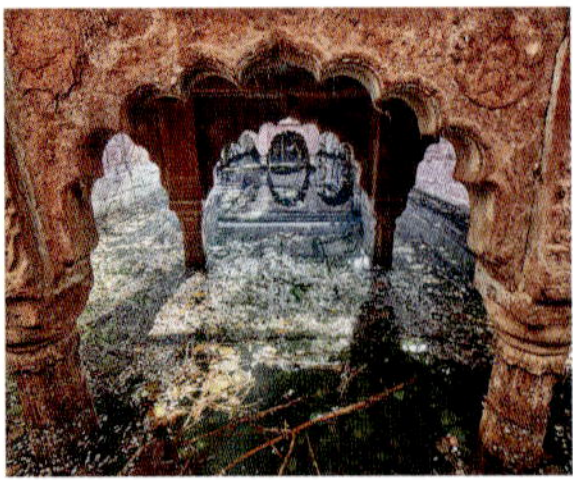

Page 23
Ram Baoli
Chandpole, Jodhpur, Rajasthan
1538 CE

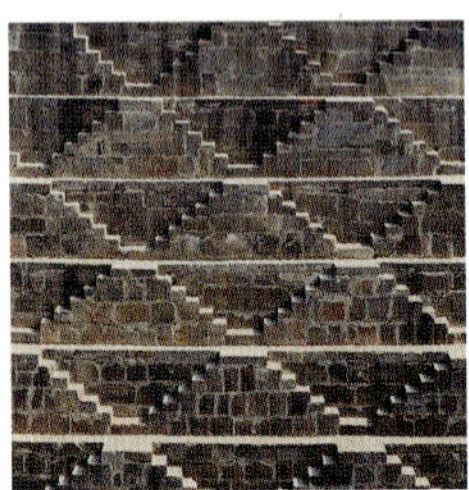

Page 24
Chand Baori
Abaneri, Rajasthan
8th-9th centuries

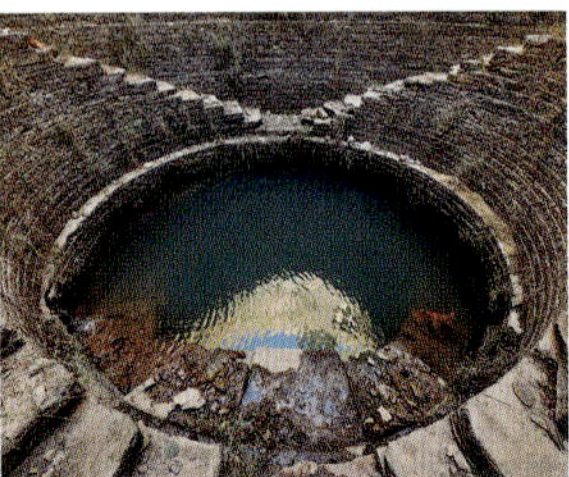

Page 25
Tapa Baoli
Chanderi, Madhya Pradesh
14th-15th centuries

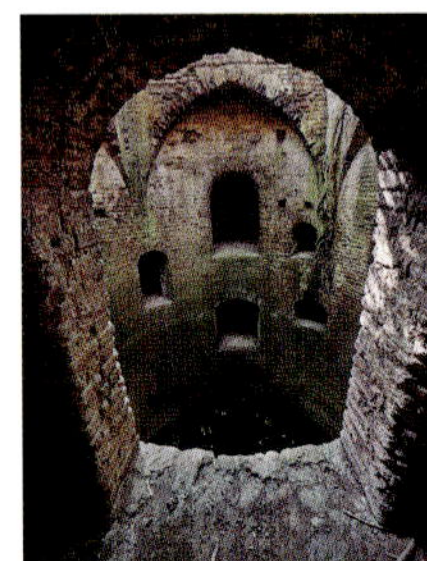

Page 26
Fer Kuo
Vasad, Gujarat
16th century

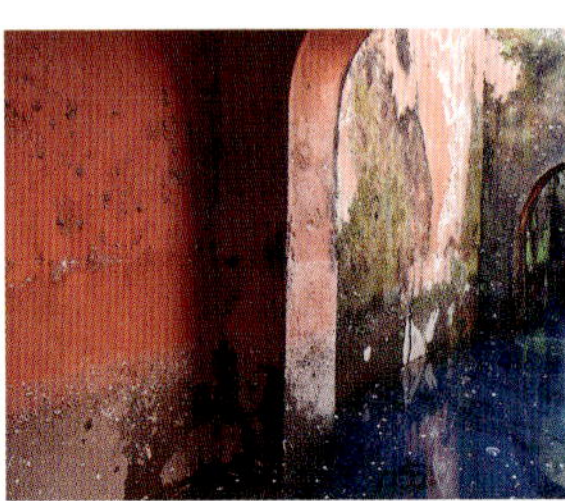

Page 27
Kamdar or Gaitore Baoli
Jaipur, Rajasthan
18th century

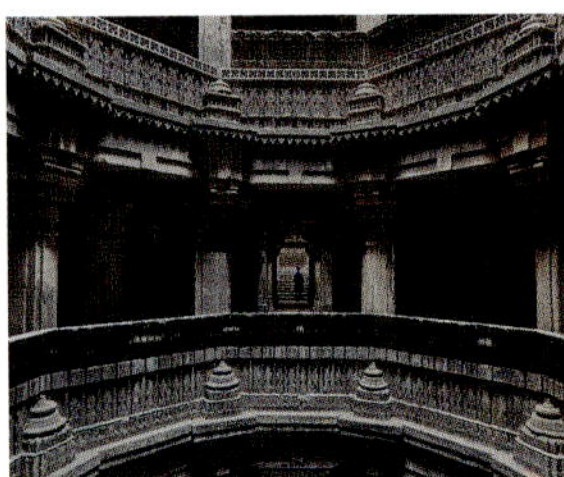

Page 29
Bai Harir Vav
Ahmedabad, Gujarat
1499 CE

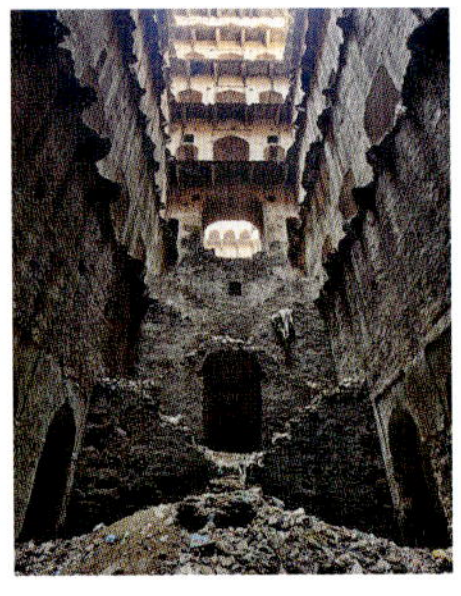

Page 30
Neemrana Baoli
Neemrana, Rajasthan
ca. 18th century

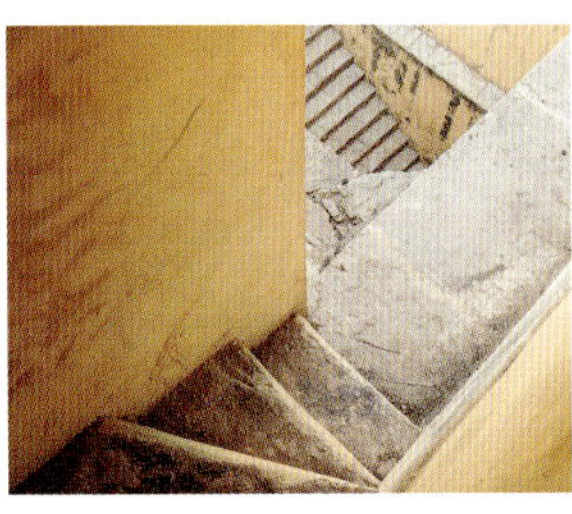

Page 32
Unnamed Vav
Amer, Rajasthan
18th century

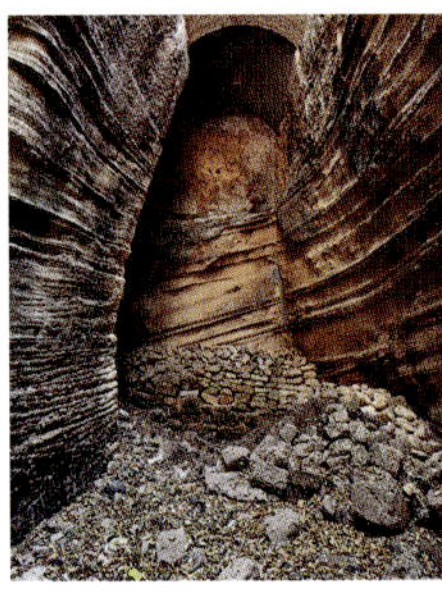

Page 33
Lashkari Vav
Junagadh, Gujarat
1st-2nd centuries CE

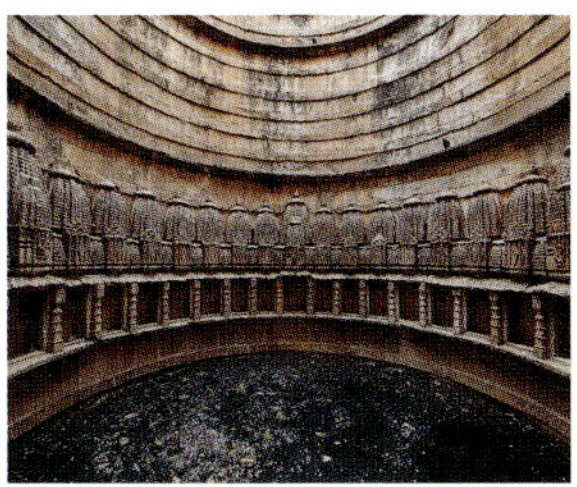

Page 34
Brahma Vav
Kedbrahma, Gujarat
14th century

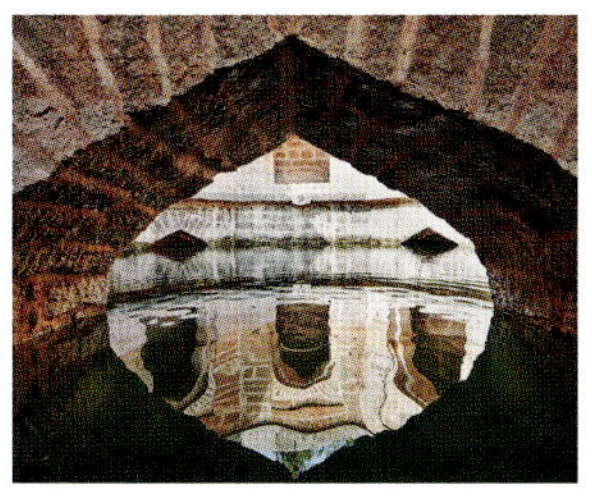

Page 35
Kuparama Vatika Kalyani
Malpangudi, Karnataka
1412 CE

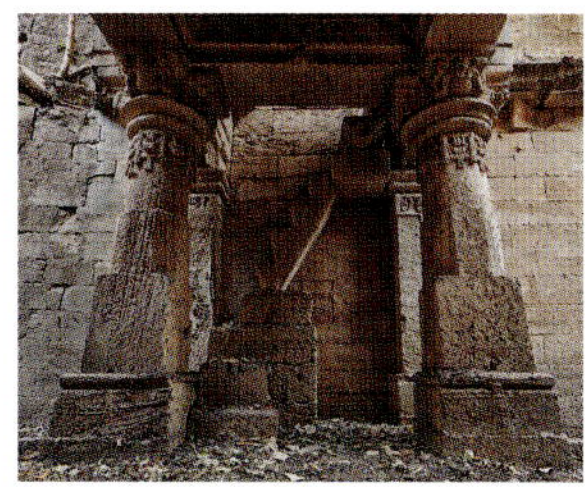

Page 36
Vikia Vav
Ghumli, Gujarat
12th-13th centuries

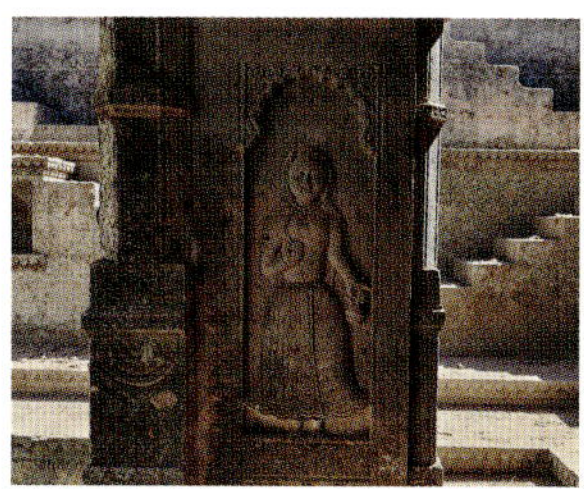

Page 37
Talab Gaon Baoli
Bundi, Rajasthan
18th-19th centuries

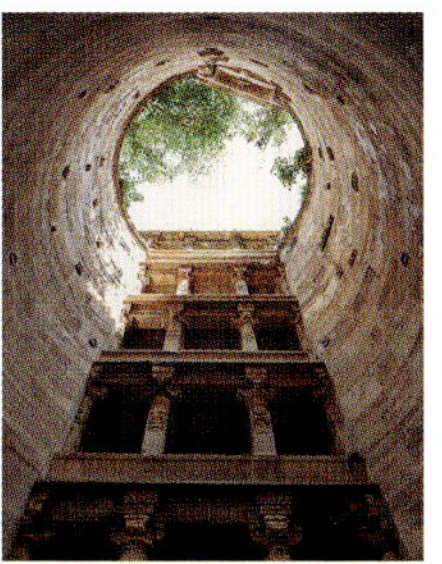

Page 39
Bahadur Singh Vav
Patan, Gujarat
19th century (using 11th-century elements from Rani Ki Vav)

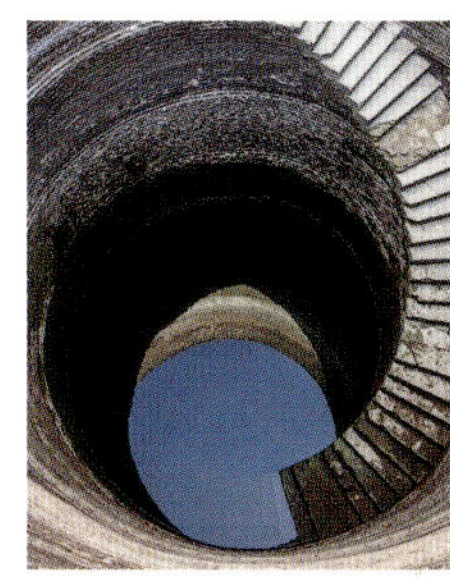

Page 40
Helical well
Champaner, Gujarat
16th century

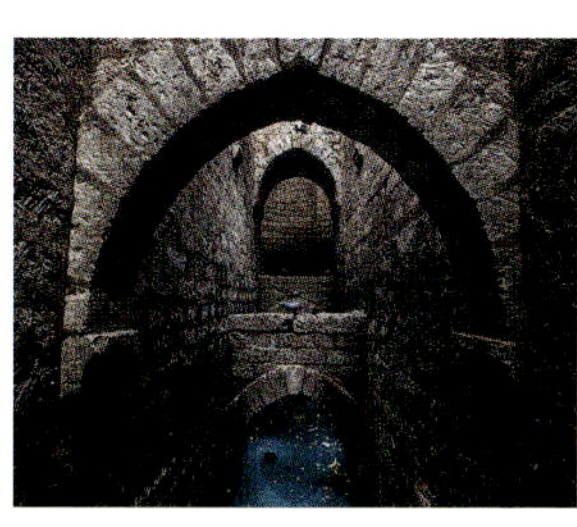

Page 41
Unnamed Vav
Mangrol, Gujarat
17-18th centuries

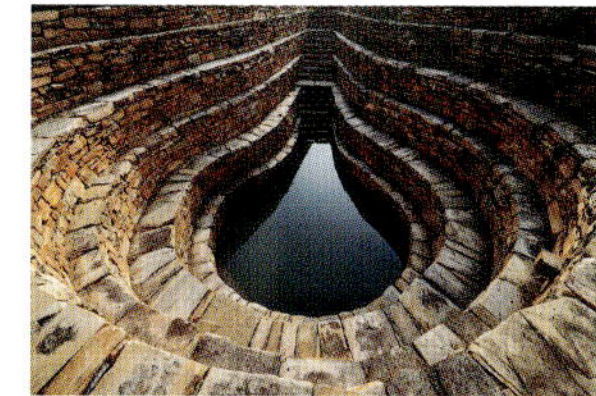

Page 43
Kund
Mailacherla, Andhra Pradesh
17th-18th centuries

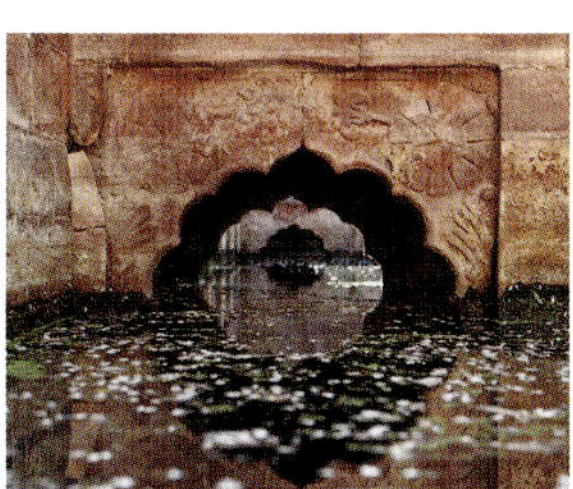

Page 45
Kund
Mailacherla, Andhra Pradesh
17th-18th centuries

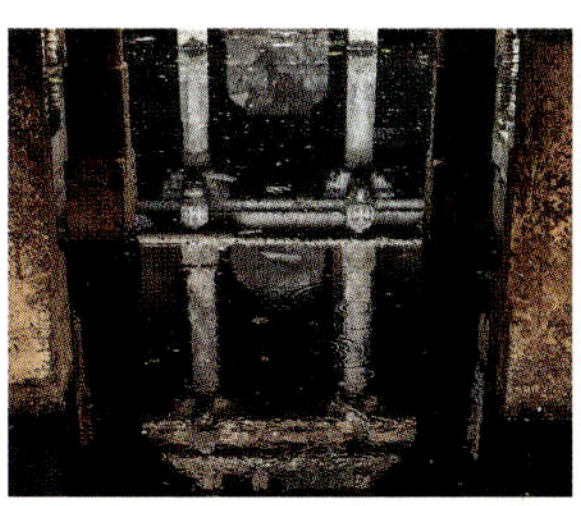

Page 46
Batris Kota Vav
Kapadvanj, Gujarat
ca. 13th century

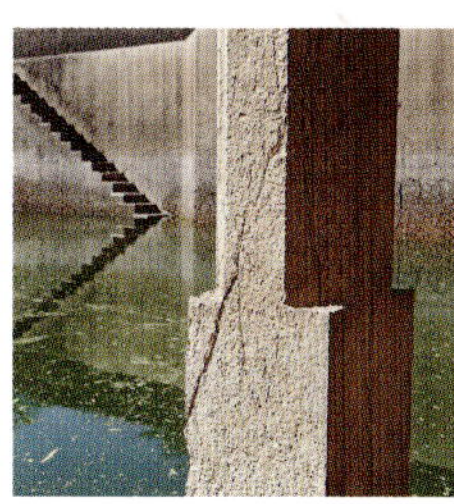

Page 48
Stepped tank above Taragarh Fort
Bundi, Rajasthan
Date unknown

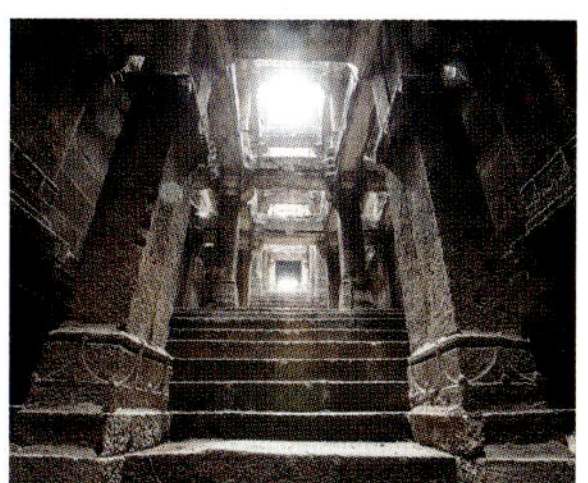

Page 49
Vidhyadhar Vav
Sevasi, Vadodara, Gujarat
1487 CE

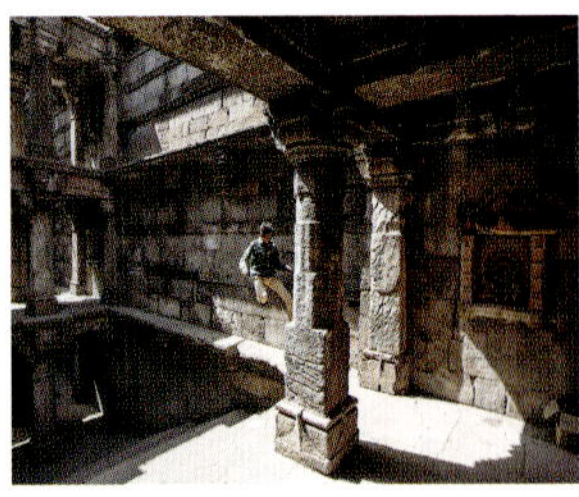

Page 50
Jetabai Vav
Ahmedabad, Gujarat
19th century (assembled using older elements from other structures)

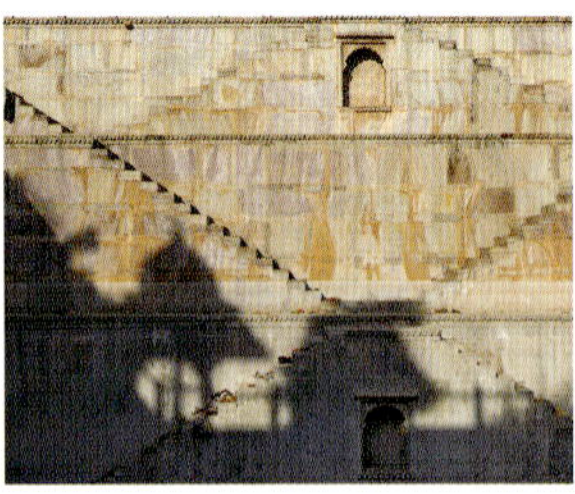

Page 51
Sagar Kund
Bundi, Rajasthan
19th century

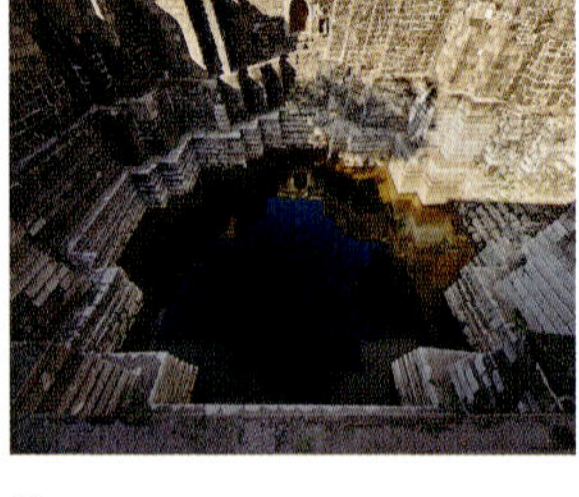

Page 53
Saraswati Kund
Devgiri Fort, Daulatabad
Maharashtra
12th-14th centuries

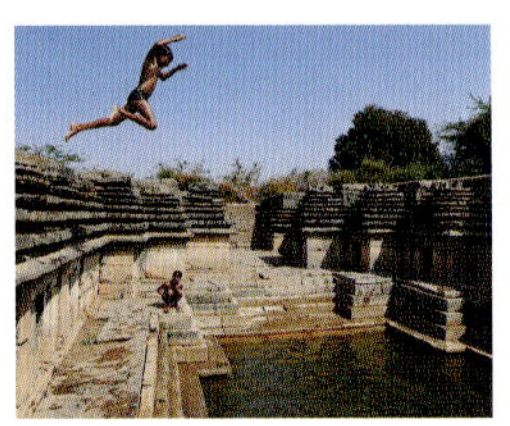

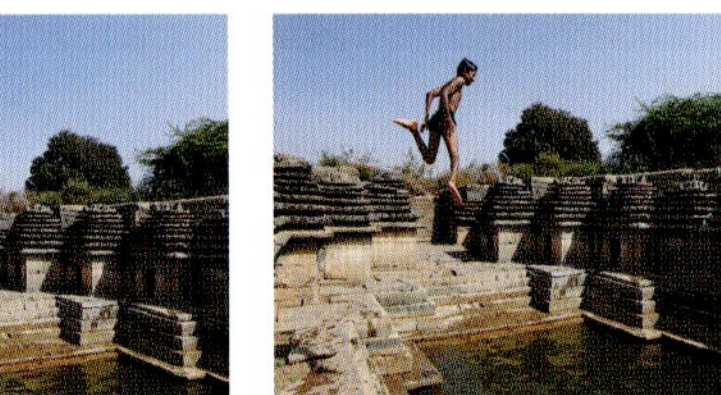

Pages 54–55
Musakeena Bhavi
Gadag, Karnataka
12th century

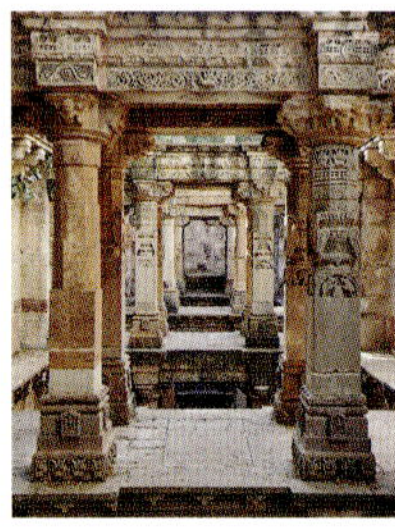

Page 56
Bahadur Singh Vav
Patan, Gujarat
19th century (using 11th-century elements from Rani Ki Vav)

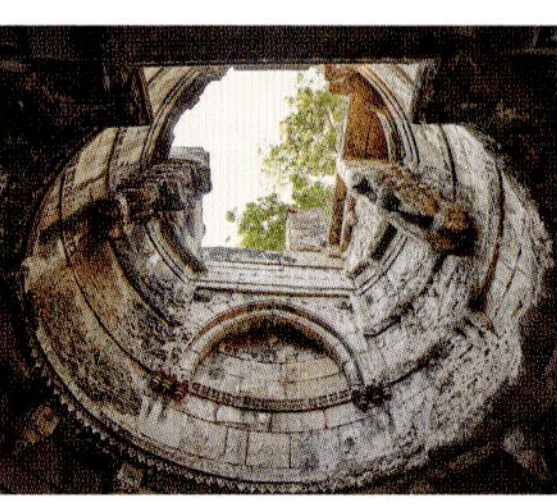

Page 57
Bai Harir Vav
Ahmedabad, Gujarat
1499 CE

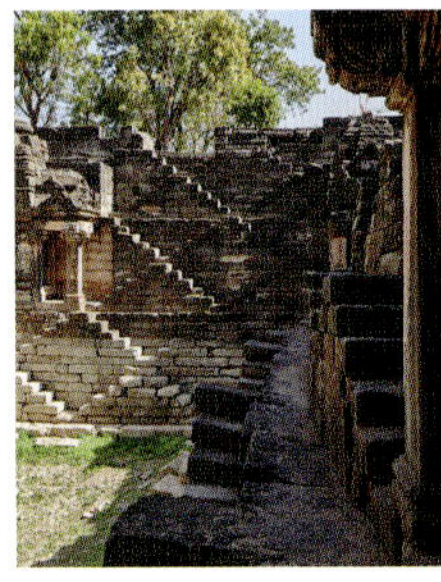

Page 58
Ladushah Kund, Roda Temple
Raisingpur, Gujarat
9th-11th centuries

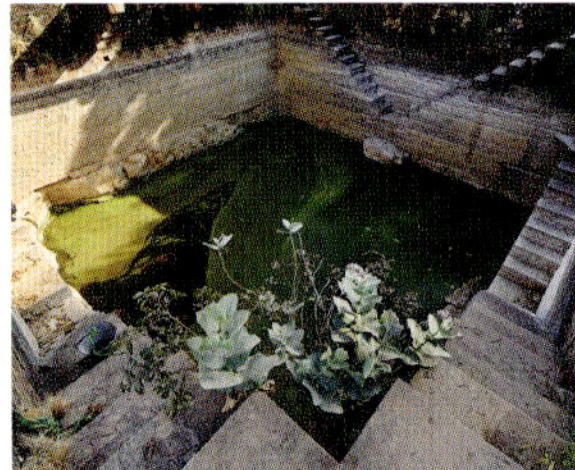

Page 59
Akola Baoli
Chanderi, Madhya Pradesh
14th-15th centuries

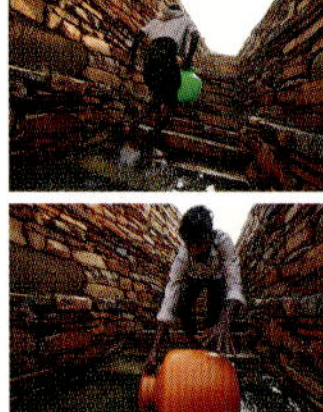

Page 61
Kund
Mailacherla, Andhra Pradesh
17th-18th centuries

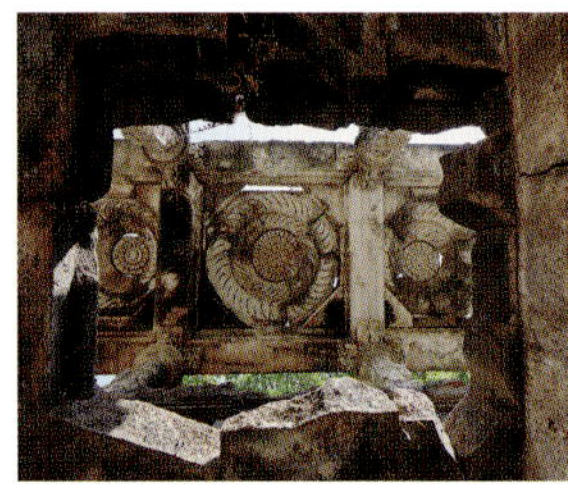

Page 62
Ankol Mata Ni Vav
Davad, Gujarat
11th century

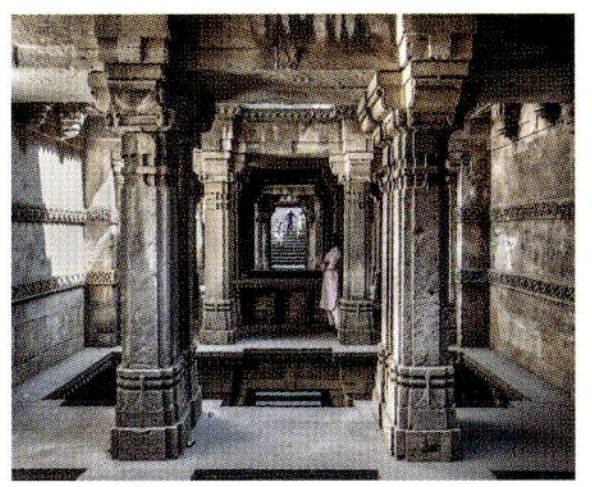

Page 63
Bai Harir Vav
Ahmedabad, Gujarat
1499 CE

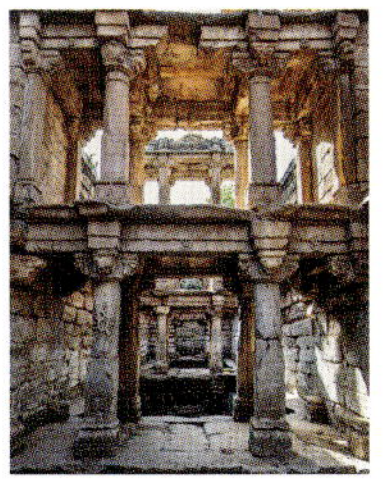

Page 64
Dhundhalanath Vav
Dhandalpur, Gujarat
13th century

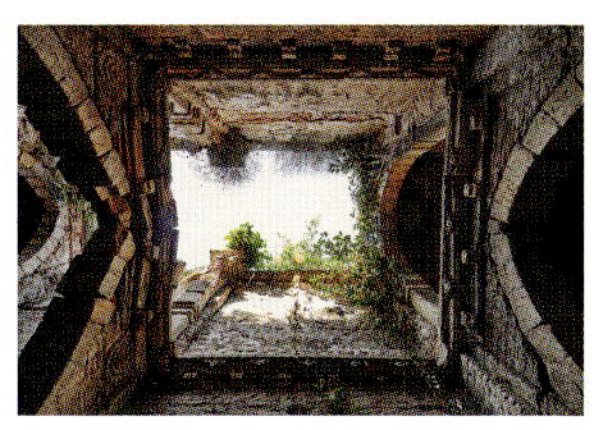

Page 65
Mahakali Maa Vav
Dholka, Gujarat
15th–16th centuries

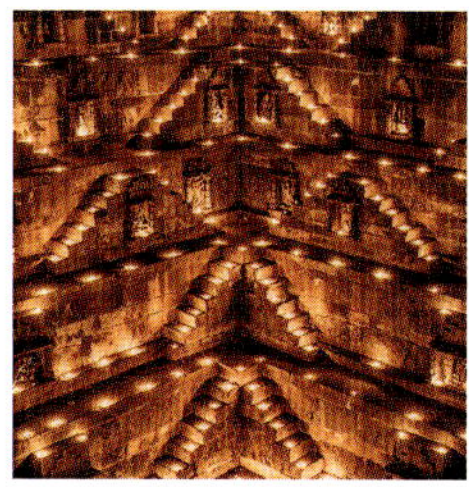

Page 67
Shakti Kund
Akhaj, Gujarat
10th century

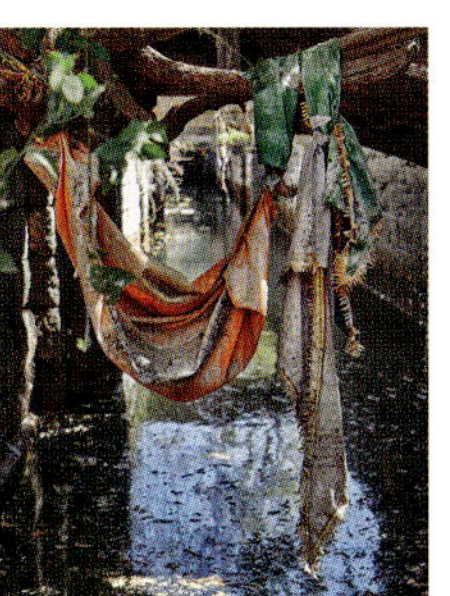

Page 68
Unnamed Vav
Near Ghumli, Gujarat
Date unknown

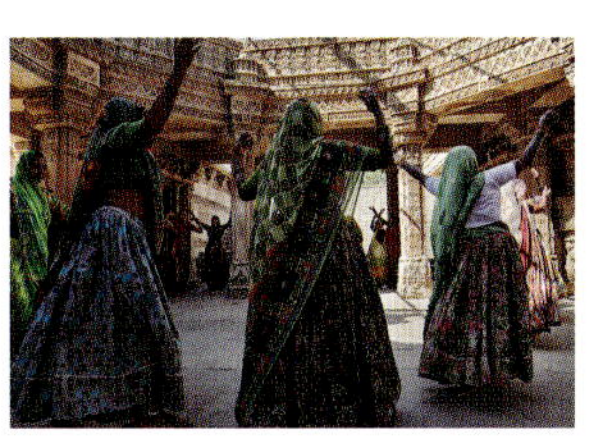

Page 71
Queen Rudabai Vav
Adalaj, Gujarat
1498 CE

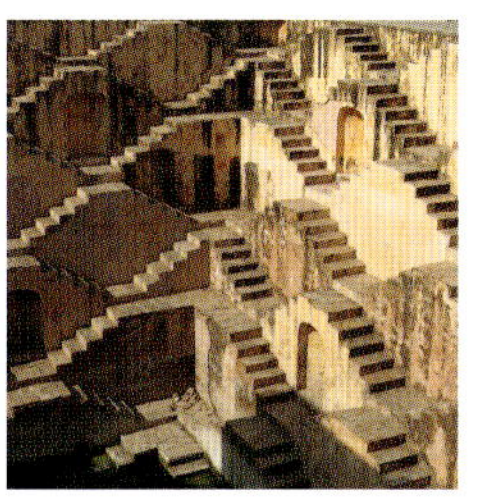

Page 95
Panna Meena Kund
Amer, Rajasthan
16th century

To see the exact location of (almost all of!) the wells photographed in this book, please flash this QR code.

Annotated Bibliography

To carry out this project, I drew on some of the abundant written and visual record of stepwells that has been compiled by historians, architects, artists, and writers over the last forty or more years. Their work reveals both the breadth of discussion of this subject and the many avenues of research that remain to be explored. I also included works by authors from other fields that I considered relevant to thinking about stepwells. These references are mainly in English. There is also an extensive corpus of research in Hindi and Gujarati that is well worth consulting.

Agarwal, Anil, and Sunita Narain, ed. *Dying Wisdom: Rise, fall, and potential of India's traditional water harvesting systems*. New Delhi: Centre for Science and Environment, 1997.
An India-wide study that situates stepwells within the larger context of the country's many water engineering practices, past, present, and future, and which highlights the magnificence and uniqueness of stepwells as water structures.

Baradi, Manvita, Meghna Malhotra, and Kaninik Baradi. *Lesser Known Stepwells In and Around Ahmedabad-Gandhinagar Region*. Ahmedabad: Urban Management Centre, 2017.
A highly instructive description and guide to the many wells in the greater Ahmedabad area, which contains several of the most beautiful in all of India.

Bhatt, Purnima Mehta. *Her Space, Her Story: Exploring the Stepwells of Gujarat*. New Delhi: Zubaan, 2014.
A pioneering and inspiring work, the first to look at stepwells as eminently female structures, from their commissioning by women to their symbolic and ritual value as a female space and their use by women as a "room of their own." If Virginia Woolf had known of stepwells …

Burtynsky, Edward. *Water.* Göttingen: Steidl, 2013.
An overview of water usage in the anthropocene era which includes a section on stepwells in Rajasthan, one of the first bodies of work to succeed in emphasizing their aesthetic dimension over their historical aspects.

Dirand, Jacques and Adrien Dirand. "The Stepwells." *SOME/THINGS, No. 5 – She Has No Strings Apollo*, (2013): 268-281.
Fresson prints of stepwells in Gujarat and Rajasthan made in 2003, the first images I ever saw of stepwells.

Earis Philip, et al., 2023. *The Stepwell Atlas.* Accessed 2021-2023, www.stepwells.org.
A website that identifies and geolocates thousands of stepwells across the Indian Subcontinent, possibly the most comprehensive such resource available online to date. It proved indispensable in my research for finding and selecting wells to photograph.

Eliade, Mircea, *The Sacred and the Profane.* Translated by Willard Trask. New York: Harcourt, 1959.
An analysis of how people sacralize their built spaces and how most constructions express a cosmogonic impulse. Eliade also elaborates on the symbolic role that the notions of ground and water play in this context, in India and elsewhere. Although he does not specifically mention stepwells, they readily conform to his analysis.

Escher, M.C, introduction by J.L. Loscher. *The Magic of M.C. Escher.* London: Thames & Hudson, 2013.
Escher is the first artist whose work comes to mind for many people (myself included) when they first see a stepwell, especially a *kund*. His process of bending spatial situations hints, formally and experientially, at the formal and structural characteristics of stepwells, even though his work focuses on closed loops, whereas stepwells are about the connectedness of multiple systems.

Hegewald, Julia. *Water Architecture in South Asia: A Study of Types, Developments and Meanings.* Leiden-Boston-Cologne: Brill, 2002.
Hegewald built on the important work done by Jain-Neubauer in Gujarat (see below) by looking at water structures across all of India.

Jain, Tanvi, Priyanka Sheth, Aashini Sheth. *Stepwells of Ahmedabad: water, gender, heritage.* Madrid-Brussels: Calmo, 2020.
An architectural study in photographs and especially drawings of the many stepwells in Ahmedabad that views them as both individual monuments and expressions of a networked engineering system and a social practice. It also reprises Purnima Bhatt's analysis of the wells as female spaces. Tanvi Jain made the beautiful drawings for this book.

Jain-Neubauer, Jutta. *The Stepwells of Gujarat: in Art-historical Perspective.* New Delhi: Abhinav Publications, 1981.
The pioneering work in modern times on stepwells, which meticulously describes the history and meaning of stepwells in the state of Gujarat.

Kale, Rohan et al. *Indian Stepwells.* Accessed 2022-2023, www.indianstepwells.com.
A website that has compiled a significant amount of information on stepwells, particularly in Maharashtra, and which is also involved in grassroots efforts and collaborations with architects to clean up and preserve stepwells.

Lautman, Victoria. *The Vanishing Stepwells of India.* London-New York: Merrell Publishers, 2017.
An excellent written and visual introduction to stepwells across India, which even includes GPS coordinates to help readers locate them. Its broad diffusion has helped draw attention to the plight of the many imperiled structures across the country.

Livingston, Morna. *Steps to Water: The Ancient Stepwells of India.* New York: Princeton Architectural Press, 2002.
This extensive, thorough description of wells and their history across India, in photographs, drawings, and text, proved the most helpful and inspiring for my research.

Masani, R.P. *Folklore of Wells, Being a Study of Water-Worship in East and West.* Mumbai: D.B. Taraporevala Sons & Co., 1918.
A comparative folkloric study of practices surrounding wells, mainly in India and the British isles. Although it deals with stepwells only very generally, the book gives some idea of their ritual value to people in India even just one hundred years ago, with a particularly vivid description of his own Parsi community in Mumbai.

Piranesi, Giovanni Battista, introduction by Mario Praz. *Le Carceri.* Milan: Abscondita, 2017.
Piranesi's "imaginary prisons," fantastical interiors with bridges and arches leading everywhere and nowhere, are formally akin to the mesmerizing architecture of certain stepwells, though different in scope.

Rössl, Stefania, photographs by Massimo Sordi. *India Water Architecture [Topos].* Siracusa: LetteraVentidue Edizioni, 2022.
A study of water systems in India and the valuable negative space they occupy in the increasingly dense public sphere in present-day India, with detailed studies of various types and systems. Its introduction also reproduces several early photographs made of stepwells in the nineteenth century by Henry Cousens, themselves rare documents, as few photographers appear to have looked into the wells during the time of British colonization. They tended to look up instead.

Van Westen, Jeroen, and Michael Pestel. *Travelogue Inverse.* Mumbai: Silverpoint Press, 2013.
A series of innovative images of stepwells and a text that probe stepwells in terms of their spatial qualities, as an ambiance, specifically how they create inverted – and not upside-down – spaces. Van Westen has also made interesting films about the dynamic experience of descending into stepwells, which may be viewed online at https://jeroenvanwesten.nl/2020/10/08/inverse-ii-films/.

And we all eagerly await the publication of Snehal Shah's magnum opus on stepwells in India, a multi-volume tome several decades in the making, with photographs by John Gollings and others!

Acknowledgments

I am grateful to many people who gave much of themselves to help me as I photographed and have made this book, and who have become a part of it as a result.

Harsh Bhavsar was initially referred to me as someone who could organize the practical details of this project for me, as I knew next to nothing about stepwells at the outset. But just a few minutes into our first conversation, it was clear to me that we would be engaging in a far more intellectually collaborative process. Over the many days spent in each other's company crisscrossing Gujarat and Rajasthan looking at wells, and in the lengthy correspondence that has ensued in between my visits to India, Harsh's eye, erudition, sensitivity, generosity, kindness, hospitality, patience, good cheer – and his ability to pick the best dhaba every time! – have informed every corner of this project; in fact, it likely would not have happened without him. I am truly grateful for his friendship. *Dhanyavaad*. For the connection to Harsh, I wish to thank Usha Bora, Zorawar Shukla, and Jaskirat Singh.

Other people soon joined this conversation. Arthur Duff has brought his boundless enthusiasm, wise counsel, and support throughout, moving mountains with his unique blend of Irish and Gujarati cheer. To my fellow travelers Ishita Jain, Noorul Khan, Manoj Shinde, Salim Chiipa, Heena Diwan, Nicole Burkhardt, Mukesh Rathore, and Krishna Chetri, your company brought great joy and camaraderie to what would otherwise have been a much more solitary journey.

My mother Marlis Zeller Cambon has been a witness to this project since its inception, standing with me at the edge of Panna Meena Kund's glowing yellow steps that sunny afternoon, and she has since supported various phases of the project, morally and financially, without which I would not have been able to carry it out so efficiently. My immense gratitude to her has only grown over time.

Lee Fontanella also mentored this project from the very first photographs to its conclusion, by providing wise guidance through not always simple terrain as he helped me edit each round of pictures from large piles of maybes to few definites, and then with the challenging task of sequencing the final images, all in the comfort of his lovely, Dots-filled home. Carl Mastandrea brought his many years of photographing and teaching to bear in advising me on making some of the final cuts, always the hardest. Thank you.

For the retouching and printing of the images, my thanks go to my old friend Hugh Milstein at Digital Fusion, Culver City for working on the first two rounds and to the team at Sheriff Paris for the third and final ones, specifically Mariette Briand, Catali Lovichi, Charlotte Cotton, Laura Rigaud, Thomas Thibaut, and especially the masterful Lina Benouhoud. Thank you for getting the images to become more themselves!

I am grateful to the incredibly talented Tanvi Jain for her gorgeous drawings, which contribute something very special to this book. For the reference to Tanvi, I wish to thank Riyaz Tayyibji of Anthill Design in Ahmedabad.

It has been a joy to watch Katarina Lang yet one more time as she brought her ever expert eye and refined sensibility to the book's design, which is so compelling and elegant to me precisely because it has so much of her in it. A friendship has been born of these books that I treasure.

A number of people read my text and offered suggestions and edits, rolling up their sleeves and getting into the nitty gritty to nudge me towards the final draft: again, Lee Fontanella, Brittain Smith, Andrew Clason, and Sherrod Blankner. Linda Connor was a source of wonderful ideas and references. My thanks go to Michelle Valladares for her many ideas, which showed me how to finish my essay, and to Rosmarie Waldrop for her suggestions of water-related poetry (with a special mention for Keith Waldrop, still in our hearts). Snehal Shah, Jutta Jain Neubauer, Julia Hegewald, and Mahesh Chandra Bora generously provided historical information and insight, in addition to their inspiring example.

Dan Schrag and Sally Stein have pointed the way to many exhibition and funding opportunities; their belief in my work means everything to me. I am also grateful to Mary Sansalone for her support and encouragement.

To Mark Sprecher, thank you for the lovely author's portrait and the wonderful afternoon on which it was made.

At ORO Editions, I am grateful to Gordon Goff and Federica Ewing for giving this project a home, and to Kirby Anderson for all her assistance in managing the production process (and for letting me keep the en dashes!). I also wish to thank Bipin Shah at Mapin for considering my work.

Many people lent a hand as I photographed. Ketan Fiske went out of his way to set me up in Nagpur at the last minute. Ramu Kotakam in Bangalore offered terrific advice, and Vishwanath Srikantaiah was very generous with his time in explaining Bangalore's water policy and connecting me to Gramer Vikas, where I am grateful to Mr. Rao, Girija Ji, and Ramakrishna Gowda for their warm welcome in Kolar District. Many thanks to Indrajeet Sawant and Shama Pawar at Kishkinda Trust for their hospitality and good company in Anegundi. Suresh and Glenice Bhavsar hosted me in Baroda and made the best kichuri I have ever eaten; I count the days until my return! Ashwin Hegde gave me a t-shirt with a *kund* motif that I still happily wear. To Raghavendra Joshi, Chetan and Anusha Bhagat, and Shalini Raghavan for lunches and dinners that buoyed my spirits, thank you.

I am most grateful to the extended Barua-Mehta-Ribeiro-Bora clan for giving me a home in so many places, from Delhi to Kasauli, Mumbai, and Bangalore, always receiving me with open arms and a smile, with a special thank you to Nila Mehta and Remani Barua for their generosity and wonderfully incorrigible habit of force-feeding me so deliciously every time!

My family and friends have been a huge source of support, as always. Their enthusiasm, feedback, and encouragement have sustained me throughout this entire process. For my birthday in 2019, friends raised money to help fund the second round of photographing, and many of them and others also bought prints from me in the fall of 2023 to fund a significant portion of the production costs.

For providing inspiring examples while I worked, because they make beautiful things that make the world a better place, I wish to thank Maneesh Jagdish, Sherrod Blankner, Luca Vacchelli, Esther David, Jeroen van Westen, Ayaan "Paper" Ribeiro, Linda Connor, Fakira Chaudhari, Nicola Canistro, Steve Faigenbaum, Reema Kagti, Carl Mastandrea, Rajesh and Payal Pratap Singh, Usha Bora, Manish Arora, and Catherine Levy, still missed.

With a special debt of gratitude to my Tante Nancy Dorian, who provided such a shining example of how joyous field work can be when you keep your heart wide open.

For everyone who pointed me to a well, who went looking for the person with keys to unlock a gate, or who otherwise expressed their kindness to me as I roamed about, thank you. Your serenity made its way into these photographs.

And, lastly, to Deeya, Elisa, and Xenia, bright stars in my sky, know that we make books not just for you, but also because of you.

Le Héron, June 2024

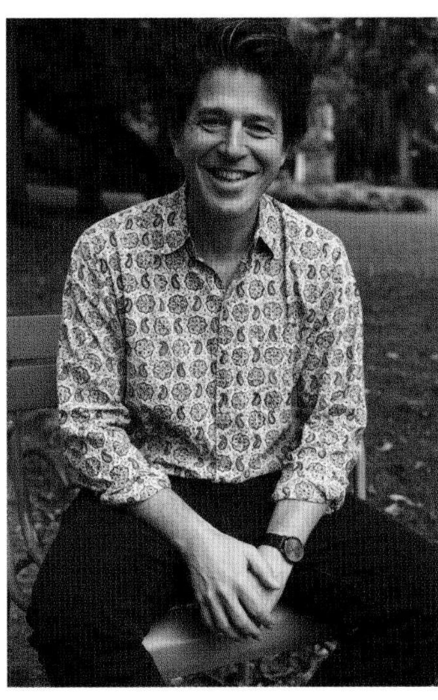

Claudio Cambon has worked as a documentary photographer for over 30 years, and for more than 25 of them in the Indian Subcontinent. He has exhibited, published, taught, and lectured across the world. His first book, *Shipbreak*, was published by Edition Patrick Frey, Zurich in 2015. He lives between Paris and rural Normandy in France.

Author photograph by Mark Sprecher

Colophon

Publishers of Architecture, Art, and Design
Gordon Goff: Publisher

www.oroeditions.com
info@oroeditions.com

Published by ORO Editions

Graphic Design: Katarina Lang Book Design
Text: Claudio Cambon
ORO Managing Editor: Kirby Anderson

First Edition

Library of Congress data available upon request. World Rights: Available

ISBN: 978-1-961856-34-9

Fonts: Bembo Std, GT Alpina, GT America Condensed
Color Separations and Printing: ORO Editions, Inc.
Printed in China.

International Distribution: www.oroeditions.com/distribution

ORO Editions makes a continuous effort to minimize the overall carbon footprint of its publications. As part of this goal, ORO Editions, in association with Global ReLeaf, arranges to plant trees to replace those used in the manufacturing of the paper produced for its books. Global ReLeaf is an international campaign run by American Forests, one of the world's oldest nonprofit conservation organizations. Global ReLeaf is American Forests' education and action program that helps individuals, organizations, agencies, and corporations improve the local and global environment by planting and caring for trees.